ABOUT THE AUTHOR

Charles Loades was born and brought up in his mother's village school house in rural Suffolk. He qualified as a teacher in 1934, at the age of 20, and went on to hold various teaching posts and Headships in different parts of London over the next forty years. As Headmaster from 1967 of one of the first Comprehensive schools in the UK - a new concept of secondary education introduced amid much controversy by the government of the day - he oversaw the creation and establishment of Creighton School in the North London Borough of Haringey, a mixed secondary school of 1500 pupils, hailed as a model of Comprehensive education in its time.

On his retirement in 1974 Charles Loades moved back to East Anglia, where he now lives in Mundesley-on-Sea, Norfolk. In addition to having been a Local Magistrate in Norfolk and Chairman of the Parish Council, he started the annual Mundesley Music Festival, which celebrates its 25th Anniversary in August 2009.

- BORN -
TEACHER

BY CHARLES LOADES

MEMOIRS OF THE FIRST 60 YEARS,
1914 TO 1974

Published 2009 by arima publishing

www.arimapublishing.com

ISBN 978 1 84549 387 5

Printed and bound in the United Kingdom

Typeset in Garamond 11

arima publishing
ASK House, Northgate Avenue
Bury St Edmunds, Suffolk IP32 6BB
t: (+44) 01284 700321

www.arimapublishing.com

CONTENTS

BORN TEACHER
FOREWORD

When it was suggested by my son and daughter-in law, Geoffrey and Sussi, that I should write the story of the first 60 years of my life, and particularly my teaching years, I was very doubtful about whether it was worth doing, or indeed whether I could remember all the incidents that might be of interest to the reader. I had not kept a diary, so it all had to come from memory. Once I set my mind to it, though, I was surprised, at the age of 94, just how strong the memories still are. Luckily, even my long-term memory is good, so I have enjoyed being able to recall in some detail the events and experiences of the 1920s and '30s, as well as my career in teaching through to the mid-1970s.

I have called the book "Born Teacher", not because of my ability to teach, but because my whole life has been associated in one way or another with teaching. My brother, sister and I were all born in the house attached to a small village school in the middle of the Suffolk countryside where our mother was the local Headmistress, so from the start we never knew any other life. I think I must have gone into the Infants Class as soon as I could walk, and I don't remember learning to read or write, or do sums. Our year was based on 'Terms' and this continued until I retired at 60. In fact, I still think now which Term we are in. It's nice to know that for most of my life I had twelve weeks holiday a year.

I'm afraid there might seem rather a lot of "I did this…" and "I did that…" in my account, but that's how it was. Of course, ideas were constantly being put forward by the Staff of the various schools, but I had to decide which ones we would use. Fortunately, we agreed about almost everything, and on only one or two occasions did I have to say "No".

One thing I did realize whilst writing these memoirs was that I had lived through a quite remarkable 60 years! Two World Wars and a revolutionary change in the education system in Britain would have been quite enough, but there was 'New Thinking' and 'New Living' as well, mainly due to the remarkable inventions during those years. There was wireless, television, international travel by land, sea and air available to far greater numbers of people that ever before, not to mention space travel and even a man landing on the Moon. New ideas were born almost daily, and so we came more recently to the computer and the mobile phone. There are those that will argue that some inventions were not beneficial and only brought new problems. I can only say that I wish I had had a computer then to do my Timetable for me!

In the 30 years since 1974 when I retired, the world has changed even more. Certainly, education is in a state of flux and I'm not sure I would like to be a teacher now – but I loved my work so much that I expect I would have taken the new ideas in my stride. I still hear from some members of my Staff at the William Grimshaw and Creighton Schools – and indeed a few pupils as well! If any others happen to read the book, I should be delighted to hear from them too.

Most of the names of people and places in the book are true. In a very few cases, they have been changed in case I might cause offence.

Hope you enjoy your read.

Charles Loades, April 2009.

ACKNOWLEDGEMENTS

My thanks are due to Geoffrey and Sussi for their encouragement. Geoffrey has done much of the editing and preparation work, which I could not have done myself.

I am tremendously grateful also to Adrienne Edwards, who patiently typed the original manuscript from my handwritten script as well as numerous revisions as it developed over several weeks and months, to Silvia Graf Jilinski who turned the manuscript into a digital text, and to Terry Palmer and Frank Rhodes for their support and assistance in various other ways.

Charles Loades

BORN TEACHER

Chapter 1
FORNHAM ALL SAINTS SCHOOL

The School, with Head Teacher's House attached, stood halfway up a hill on the road that ran from Fornham All Saints to the village of Westley, crossing the main Newmarket-to-Bury road on the way.

Built in 1870 and called Fornham All Saints Board School, it served the pupils from both villages and was probably named after Fornham because it was the larger of the two. Each village was a mile away. There was no transport and the pupils walked to school and back in all weathers, thinking nothing of their two-mile journey each day. In the distance, two miles away, one could see Bury St. Edmunds, the main town of West Suffolk, where all our shopping had to be done.

Of course the school was constructed of flint - the primary building material in that part of Suffolk, because the stones could easily be dug up from the surrounding fields. Even today, although overgrown, the pits can be seen which supplied the stone. Completely waterproof, the flint could be used as single stones or 'knapped' – split in half, to show the attractive shiny black inside. Flint 'knapping' had been a craft in that part of Suffolk for hundreds of years and is still practised today. The road connecting the villages was also made of flint. Each year, a steam-roller would press in more stones to fill the potholes – not the best of surfaces for traffic but in those days cars were few and far between. In our village, the Rector, three farmers and the so-called 'Squire' were the only people to own one. You either walked or you rode a bicycle!

The school must have been a very impressive building at that time. It had one large classroom for the 60 or so children between 7 and 11 years old who were divided into classes but still all taught by the Headmistress, with occasional help from a 'Supply' or 'Student Teacher'. At age 11, they took an examination and passed on to schools in Bury St. Edmunds – some to Grammar and others to the Secondary Schools.

A smaller room housed the infants, aged 5 to 7, with their own teacher – I remember her well, Mrs. Crimmings – a very good violinist – who accompanied the whole school for Country Dancing, in which we all joined.

There were separate cloakrooms for girls and infants together, and for the boys. No running water was available so large pails of water stood by the sinks. I don't think anyone washed very much.

The large tarred playground, surrounded by lime trees, gave plenty of room for games. The infants had their own small playground.

Toilets were provided in both playgrounds and were simple in the extreme, being buckets under a wooden seat in a hut divided up into cubicles. They were emptied by being pulled out through small doors at the back. As Caretaker, this was the job of my Grandfather each day and our large garden benefited from the results – we had the best gooseberries for miles around!

The School House was quite roomy. Downstairs was a parlour – used only on Sundays and when visitors came; and a sitting/dining room where we ate and spent our time indoors reading or playing table games. This room also had a coal- heated range with an oven, and here all the cooking was done. A large black kettle stood on the stove at all times and provided hot water all day long. It was a very cosy room and we spent many happy hours there.

From the sitting room you passed into the scullery, which contained a coal-fired boiler used on Washing Days, a mangle and a sink. On the boiler, when it was not being used, was a large white enamel bucket, which contained the fresh water from the hand-pump in the yard outside. We never seemed to do anything to the water – just drank it as it came from the pump – and we never had any ill effects that I know of.

The one-and-only toilet was outside in the yard. Again, it was a container under a wooden seat, a bucket of water nearby and yesterday's "Daily Mirror" torn into strips as toilet paper. It was emptied every day into the garden.

The only other downstairs room, and it was quite large, was a walk-in pantry. Being so isolated, as we were, much of our food was bought in reasonably large quantities. The pantry was cool and roomy. Grandfather provided all the vegetables and mother cycled or walked to Bury with us on Saturdays to get the groceries. Only one bus a week ran on the Newmarket Road on a Saturday morning and the bus-stop was at least half a mile away so it was not worth using.

Upstairs were three bedrooms. In one slept my mother and father, in the second my grandfather and me in a double bed, and my brother in a single. My sister had the small bedroom. Our washing and other needs were served by a washbasin and jug, and a jerry under the bed.

As you will gather, we had none of the 'necessities' of modern life but never felt deprived.

Oil lamps lit the downstairs rooms, and candles the bedrooms at night. There was no telephone. We considered that this was the normal way of life as we had no experience of anything else. We often had visitors to stay but I cannot remember any criticism – I expect they took this as being ordinary country life.

Chapter 2
THE FAMILY

My mother must have been a very young teacher when she became Headmistress. Obviously her organizational and leadership abilities were apparent at an early age. You received your teacher training in a school where you were sent to help out, immediately you left your own school at the age of 13.

Because of this, you were thrown in at the deep end, taking charge of pupils almost the same age as yourself. If you were going to make a Teacher you were soon made aware of it and went on to gain your Teacher's Certificate.

The First World War began on the 4th of August, 1914. I was born on the 20th. There was no connection between the two events, I can assure you. In fact, I don't remember any of those War Years at all. Living in the depths of the countryside, as we were, I don't suppose that is surprising. I do have a faint memory of being held in a woman's arms on a bridge over a river with a man beside us. The woman said, "If you don't stop crying I'll throw you into the water!" I can only imagine it was mother seeing my father off to join his regiment abroad. I know he was in the Royal Artillery and I can hardly believe she would say such a thing, but I expect she was worried and desperate at seeing him go.

I don't remember him coming home on leave and he never once talked of his war experiences in his life. I wish now that I had asked him more about them.

My mother and father were busy people, both in their public and their private lives. We called them 'Mum' and 'Dad' and certainly lived as a family. We all knew what everybody else was doing and where they were. Nobody seemed to have secrets from each other. In fact, it was a very happy family life.

Dad's mother and father kept a pub – "The Three Goats" in Bury. When his father died, his mother, with the help of three daughters, Connie, May and Marjorie as barmaids, carried on. She was very independent and used to visit us at least one afternoon a week in her pony and trap. Often, after school, she would give us a ride part of the way back and we would walk home.

The pub had a large yard and stables. On market days, two or three 'carriers' would arrive from outlying villages with their passengers and goods, stable the horses, deliver their produce and do shopping for villagers. I went to Grandma every day for lunch when I was at the County School at Bury and these were exciting days. Market days were Wednesdays and Saturdays and I looked forward to the former. The pub would be full of people and I would be allowed to help feed the horses. I watched them being shoed and, best of all, saw the carts being 'touched up' by a painter who was skilled at doing repairs to the paintwork, freehand.

Grandma died when I was about 15 and I missed her very much. I can still taste her blackcurrent puddings with clotted cream – the latter sent all the way from Devon by a friend.

The pub is still there but is now a small block of flats.

My Dad had taken an apprenticeship in printing and was a skilled Linotype operator. He must have been good because he was offered a job by a London newspaper, but turned it down. We were all very relieved. Who wanted to leave Suffolk for London!

He worked at the local newspaper, the 'Bury Free Press', which came out on Fridays. Every morning, he travelled to Bury on his Douglas motorbike, which was used, with sidecar attached, to take the family out at the weekends. I sat on the pillion, and Mum had Mollie and Douglas sitting in front of her in the sidecar.

On Thursday nights Dad worked till midnight as the paper was printed for the Friday delivery. He was back at 8am the next morning. He brought us home the "Daily Mirror" each evening with our favourite strip cartoon – 'Pip, Squeak and Wilfred.'

When I was at school at Bury, I often called in on the way home to see him. I was fascinated by the way a Linotype machine worked. The molten metal, which made up the 'slug' on which the words were typed, hardened at the exact moment to take the print. The Linotype operator sat at a keyboard like that of a typewriter and typed in the script. Each 'slug' was the width of a newspaper column and the thickness of a letter. The operator checked that the spacing and spelling were correct and then the 'slugs' were placed in a tray by a compositor in the position they would appear on a page of the newspaper. A final check for spelling and then into the printing machine, where it was inked and then pressed onto the paper-roll, which was cut and came out as a page the other end. To this day, I have no idea how all this happened.

Dad was an easy-going man who took a great interest in what we were doing and was always prepared to take part in our activities – particularly on the sports side.

I suppose, living so far away from anyone else, we had to live as a family and this we certainly did!

Both parents took care of themselves with regard to appearance and behaviour and they made sure we did to. This was something which has stayed with us for the rest of our lives, and I still dislike unnecessarily shabby clothes, bad manners and slovenly speech. Today's television presenters make me cringe with their raucous voices and noisy music background. I suppose I must put it down to 'old age'.

You felt you could trust Mum as soon as you met her and that she could help with your troubles. Many of the village people came to her for advice and she went out of her way to try and help. She had the gift of being a good organizer – a gift that has been inherited by the family, right down to our grandchildren! There was a quiet air of authority about her, which led to confidence in her planning. Again, she loved the family and was never happier than when we were doing things together.

Granddad, Thomas Barnett, lived with us too. His wife had passed away before I was born. At 60, he was a fine strapping man who had been a village policeman. Well versed in the ways of the country, he was the School Caretaker and looked after our large vegetable garden. He would have been very upset if he could not supply us with vegetables and fruit all the year round. There was fruit in abundance, with much of it stored for the Winter.

As a policeman he had had to visit Newmarket Race Meetings, and he still wished he could go. He took us up to the Newmarket Road crossing on Race Days to see the cars coming home. A great treat for us; unless we went to Bury, we never saw a car at all.

He had been a great admirer of Fred Archer, the Champion Jockey, and named his son Archer Barnett. Over the years, this had become 'Archie' and that was how we knew our favourite uncle.

As well as looking after the garden, he kept chickens for our eggs and we always hatched new ones when we needed them. If you have never seen a baby chicken emerge from its shell, you have missed a treat. Pecking its way out, it staggers to its feet and immediately tucks into the mashed hard-boiled egg waiting for it.

When we had young chickens we often had trouble with a hawk, which would pounce through the open top of the chicken run. Granddad did quite a lot of shooting for the local farmers, when rooks fed on the newly-seeded fields and he always left a loaded shotgun standing in the scullery. We had strict orders not to touch it, although it would not fire until the breech was closed. One day, the hawk appeared. Mum, who had never fired a gun in her life, grabbed it, aimed and shot the bird dead. This was the talk of the village for weeks and Mum had a very sore shoulder.

Granddad's constant companion was a large black Labrador named Dinah. She was a wonderful dog who went with him shooting but was so gentle she could play with us. One day, in her soft mouth, she carried every egg from a pheasant nest at the top of the garden down to the mat outside the back door. She didn't break one.

I have mentioned Uncle Archie. He and his wife, and daughter Betty, who was the same age as Mollie, played a big part in our lives. They lived at Bury and came over to us most weekends. Uncle Archie worked as a secretary in the office of a motor garage and was in my eyes the ideal Uncle. He was always trying new things out or inventing things himself, and his knowledge of country lore was tremendous.

On a Sunday afternoon, when he was with us, Dad, Douglas and I always went for a long country walk and I learnt the names and uses of trees and plants, which I could not have learned in any other way. He showed me how to make a pop gun by hollowing out the pith from a short, straight piece of alder, finding a nut stem to fit it, putting half an acorn in each end and then pushing the handle in as hard as possible. The resulting air pressure would fire the acorn with a bang and leave a new piece for the next firing.

We would walk two miles to Ickworth Park and dam the small stream which ran through the grounds. We would collect discarded antlers from the many deer that roamed the park and leave them near the house. We never did any damage and nobody ever stopped us.

Archie was also the first person I knew who had a camera. He made our first wireless set with a cat's whisker and a crystal, and followed this with a valve set and an accumulator.

He took my brother and me in our best navy-blue Sunday suits to the top of a windmill. When we came down we were covered with white flour! We all three got a good telling off from Mum! Yes, we always looked forward to his visits – you never knew what was going to happen next.

So this was our family, a happy and busy one, but always centred around school and village.

Chapter 3
THE VILLAGE

Although it was Fornham All Saints School, one must not forget that it also catered for the smaller village of Westley. Because of its size, it was served by the Fornham parson and as far as I can remember there was no Village Hall so not many evening events took place. We liked to go to Church there in the Spring when all the hedges seemed full of lilacs and laburnum, and the fruit farm was alive with apple blossom.

Every Sunday we attended church at Fornham, morning and evening. In those days, some families had their own pews – the farmers, the Squire and the Head Teacher. Ours was close under the pulpit and the sermon was a painful experience, leaning back to see the parson. Father was in the choir and we boys joined him later; not Mollie though – girls were not allowed in the choir in those days.

Whatever the weather – and often in the Winter there was snow – we walked there; never cycled. Visitors had to attend with us. One Sunday, Dad's youngest brother – a bit of a dude – came to see us wearing suede shoes. There was a slight sprinkling of snow and you can imagine what his shoes looked like when we returned. He never came again on a Sunday!

I have pleasant memories of the church services, particularly the evening ones. The warm, friendly church, the flickering candles and oil lamps and a good congregation, and then the walk home in the pitch-black dark with the stars showing up so brightly overhead.

If you have never seen stars in a night sky in the country you have no idea how bright they can be. Orion, the North Star, the Plough, we knew them all. John Masefield knew what he meant when he wrote, "I must go down to the seas again, to the lonely sea and the sky, and all I ask is a tall ship and a star to steer her by."

Somehow we always seemed to finish with my favourite hymn, "The day thou gavest Lord is ended." I hope it is played for me when I pass on.

Dad was quite a sportsman and played for the football team in the Village League. He was centre-forward and always had stew with dumplings for Saturday dinner. He said that he scored the same number of goals as the dumplings he ate. He played cricket for Hengrave, as we had no team, and once bowled out nine men and caught the other – so he said. He was a good billiards player and won trophies at the Constitutional Club at Bury. I returned one of his trophies to the still existing club for their antiquities collection only a few years ago. He played tennis and bowls, and when he was a very young man used to sprint at local village sports meetings. Evidently they were quite usual in those days during the Summer and he came home with prizes. The one I remember best was a beautiful wall-clock.

We were taken by Mum to see him play football and I must have been very young. The Village Squire played in goal and wouldn't wear football togs. He appeared in his shooting jacket, breeches and cap and I never saw him in anything else.

All of us inherited Dad's ability and his love of sports, having success in various ways, which I will write about later. I do know that I was much better at hitting a moving ball than a still one. Snooker and golf were not my best games.

Mum organized events in the Village Hall, and visits out for the Church Choir and the School. During the Winter, there were dances and concerts, sales and meetings in the Hall, nearly all arranged by her. In the Summer, she had day trips out for the Church and the School. These were always to Yarmouth, which was the favourite seaside resort for us all.

The charabanc would pick us up at 7:30am for the long journey. In those days, the coach had a concertina roof, which could be folded to the back in fine weather. The weather always seemed to be good, which added to the thrill of travelling this way. Remember that for most of the village this would be the only time they would travel in a motor vehicle.

At St. Olaves, near Yarmouth, we all had to get out because the charabanc plus passengers was too heavy a load for the bridge over the river. We walked, and the empty bus followed, to be boarded again on the other side. This was extremely exciting and viewed with some fear and trepidation. I have not crossed the bridge there since those days. I wonder if you still have to alight?

Our whole day was spent on the wonderful beach, although the more elderly enjoyed the shops and amusements on the promenade. Tea was taken at a restaurant on the Front and it was always shrimps followed by fresh fruit salad – dishes we never had at home. Afterwards, a walk along the promenade and a go on the penny-in-the-slot machines would bring us to Britannia Pier and the coach. The boys had the back seat, where we could kneel and throw paper streamers as we passed cyclists. They enjoyed it as much as we did and would pedal furiously to keep up.

As darkness fell, the roof was closed and we settled down for a good sing along – the song "Bye-Bye Blackbird" was the favourite of those days – I can still remember the words and tune. Gradually tiredness took over and most of us were asleep by the time we reached home. Happy days!

Mum was quite ambitious in her choice of trips. The School even went to the Annual Aldershot Tattoo on Salisbury Plain and the Commonwealth Exhibition at Wembley, which had just been built. The latter was in the early twenties and I particularly remember it because the Rector gave a book, "Clive of India", as prize for the best essay on the trip, and I won it - on merit, I might add; not favouritism to the Head-teacher's son!

Chapter 4
HOME & SCHOOL

Unlike the other children, for this small four-year-old boy, going to school in the first week of September, 1918, was no new experience. As I have said, in our lives the two buildings, home and school, merged into one.

What he did not know was that he was entering the world of education, which in some form or other he would be in for the next 56 years of his life!

He already knew how to use a slate. He would not use paper till later when he had mastered the skill of writing. A slate was so handy. Make a mistake, and a wet rag would wipe it away in a moment.

I do not remember learning to read or write, or my time in the 'infants' but the junior school was another matter. I already had a baby brother and soon would have a sister. They were looked after during the day in the house by a young former pupil. She was paid two shillings and sixpence a week. This left Mum free to concentrate on her teaching.

I always think that she invented school meals! The large room was heated by a coal fire, with a fire guard round it of course. During the Winter a large cauldron full of water was suspended over the fire. The children would each bring a vegetable from their gardens to school each morning and this would be washed and dropped into the container. Mum would add a few spoonfuls of meat extract and there it simmered till lunchtime.

Out came the mugs and there was hot soup to eat with our sandwiches. We had our main meal with Dad when he got home in the late afternoon.

The school day always began with Assembly – a Hymn and a Prayer and some news to take home to parents. Mum was a good pianist and made sure that the children sang well too. She had a choir which sang at concerts and excelled itself one year by winning the Choral Group for School Choirs at the Suffolk Music Festival. I was in that choir, and the excitement was intense when we arrived home with the banner, which hung in the hall for the next year.

Once a week the Rector would come and take Assembly, as we were a Church School. I was told that the following story originated at our school, but I don't believe it.

After Assembly the Rector usually gave a talk. This day he asked, "Who knocked down the Walls of Jericho"?
There was dead silence so he fixed his eyes on one small boy and said: "Don't you know"?
The boy said, "No sir, but I didn't".
The shocked Rector went to my mother and told her the story. He said, "It was the small ginger headed boy in the front row."
My mother replied, "He's a very truthful boy – if he said he didn't, he didn't."
Even more shocked the Rector went to see the Chairman of School Governors. He listened intently and said: "Don't worry Rector. We've plenty of money in the school funds this year – we'll build them up for you!"

After Assembly we all recited our twelve times table. Nobody left Fornham School without knowing their multiplication tables and I didn't know anyone who could not read.

Country dancing was very popular and we all learned to dance. Mrs Crimmings accompanied us on the violin and we always danced at school concerts. Mum was so keen on concerts that she had the village blacksmith make her a portable stage, which filled a quarter of the Hall from wall to wall and could be stored away until needed. He also made me my first iron hoop!

Occasionally, to raise money for the school, she would put on an evening dance. The Hall was cleared of everything and the wooden floors sprinkled with French Chalk to make them smooth. A small band provided the music and people came from far and wide.

In a corner of the Hall stood a Nature Table and we were encouraged to bring suitable objects to be placed there for all to see. It was surprising what turned up sometimes!

As you will have gathered, personal hygiene was a bit of a problem, but every Friday evening we children had our weekly bath.

In the Summer there were so many flies settled on the sitting room ceiling that they had to be cleared so they didn't fall in the bath. Dad would go round with a glass of paraffin holding it tight against the ceiling and the flies would just fall off into the glass. When I was tall enough, the duty fell to me.

The procedure was always the same. The large tin bath was placed in front of the kitchen range and filled with hot water from the copper. There was an advertisement at the time that said "Friday night is Amami night." Amami was a shampoo, and certainly used by us.

The order of bathing was – Mollie, Doug and me. We sat in the bath and were thoroughly sponged all over, then dried in front of the fire. If we had the semblance of a cold, Vick ointment was rubbed on our chests and Thermogene, a sort of fine wool pad, was applied. As the cold gradually went, pieces were torn off the pad until we were clear. Finally, a spoonful of California Syrup of Figs was swallowed and we were right for another week.

With the warmth from the range and the flickering lamplight, this was an evening to savour till we took candles and went drowsily to bed.

In the Winter with the wind howling outside and snow piling up on the windowsills, as it did every year, it was even better.

From the age of 8, I was given the job of collecting our milk from Charley Brown's farm in Fornham. I would walk down with the pupils going home, carrying my two-pint can, but my journey back was on my own. This was fine in the Summer but the walk back in the dark was quite an adventure. Two groups of elm trees stood on the high parts of the road and they creaked and groaned in the wind. I usually scurried under them but I cannot say I ever felt frightened and there was never anyone about except the occasional farm labourer returning home on his Suffolk Punch. What magnificent horses they are!

We all learned to cycle at an early age and soon I could carry the milk can on my handlebars. In the Winter, this meant having a bicycle lamp. Bikes had a red reflector on the back mudguard but most people used a Carbide lamp - and very ingenious they were too! The container at the base was filled with Carbide powder and the top with water. When turned on, the water, drop by drop, fell on the carbide below and made a flammable gas which fed the burner. The gas was lighted with a match as it issued through the burner with a glass front. The resulting light was not very strong but at least it let people know you were there.

We were very glad indeed when the Dynamo, driven by the bike's front wheel, was invented. It saved a lot of trouble and worry.

I am sad to say that the elm trees are no longer there. They fell victim to the Dutch Elm Disease that swept the country in the '70s.

As a matter of interest, have you ever tried swinging a full can of milk round your head to show the effect of centrifugal force? I was quite good at it and only once had to use my meagre pocket money to buy two pints of milk. By the way, haven't times changed? Can you imagine a child of 8 being out all by himself on a lonely road on a Winter's evening nowadays?

As I have said, Mum was a good pianist and we were all given the chance to have piano lessons. A small Welshman with a Triumph 3-Wheeler and a limp came to us once a week after school. He was a good teacher and we all learned to play to a reasonable standard. Mollie was quite brilliant, and passed all her exams up to the highest grade.

Exams were held at the Atheneum at Bury in the middle of Winter and usually we cycled there on a Saturday morning. These days stay in my mind because you always arrived frozen stiff and had to put your hands in a basin of hot water to get the feeling back. Good preparation for a piano exam!

Later I had to go to a teacher at Bury. I don't remember his teaching but I know he was the uncle of Amy Johnson when she was famous for her airplane flights. I enjoyed the effect of the reflected glory among my schoolmates.

We never seemed to have serious illnesses. German measles were quite common but I never heard of anyone suffering from the effects. Our one crisis was when Douglas and I had Scarlet Fever together in the middle of the Summer. The doctor said, much to our dismay, "Off to the Isolation Hospital at Bury for six weeks", but Mum had other ideas. She had a tent erected on our lawn, well away from the house, and promised that no one but she would visit us.

It was a beautiful Summer and as neither of us felt ill we thoroughly enjoyed the experience. We had school work to do, slept on air mattresses and washed in bowls of water brought to us. Everything was disinfected after use and there were no more outbreaks of the fever.

Often we would lie on our backs on the grass and just watch the sky. It was then I discovered the wonderful cumulus clouds that floated above us. These white cotton-wool formations are not seen anywhere else but in Suffolk and Norfolk, I suppose because of the land formation. I still enjoy them from the garden today.

So the years passed by and we suddenly realized that I would be 11 years old next August and would be taking the exam which would decide my future school. I was fortunate to be born in August because in education everything was organized from the 1st of September. It is the start of a new school year that you are entering at the youngest possible age. Somebody with a birthday in late September will always have to wait another year before making a move that can be quite important in some professions. This was a crucial time in my life.

The examination questions for the 11-plus arrived at school well before the end of Term and all schools sat it on the same day. Papers were marked by the Staff and returned to the Education Office. Then it was a case of waiting for the results and seeing to which school we would move.

I found I had passed and would be attending the West Suffolk County School in September as a paying pupil. It meant little to me at the time. Summer holidays were much more important. On our return from these, it came as something of a shock to me that for the first time in my life I was going to be away from home in a strange school with people I didn't know. What would it all be like?

Chapter 5
SUMMER HOLIDAYS

There is no doubt that the high point of each year was the six weeks of Summer holiday. It was the only time when Dad had two continuous weeks of holiday and we could all spend it together.

From the time when we were old enough to go to the seaside, the pattern was always the same – two weeks at home, two weeks at Yarmouth or Gorleston, and the last fortnight at home. This continued until I was 20 and left College – real family holidays that we never failed to enjoy.

We were surrounded by cornfields in Suffolk and the harvest was in full swing when the holiday began. From as long as I can remember, we children spent the first two weeks in those cornfields.

Immediately after breakfast, lunch would be packed; a hunk of bread, a slice of cheese and an onion, an apple and a bottle of Eiffel Tower lemonade. How the latter got its name I don't know, but it was made of green crystals dissolved in water and was delicious.

The weather always seemed to be sunny so there was no need for coats. We all wore Clarks sandals with no socks and the first few days were very painful. The stubble in the fields cut into our bare ankles and we sat with our feet in bowls of warm water, laced with iodine, during the evenings. After three days, the skin had hardened, the cuts healed and we had no more trouble.

The men had started work when we arrived. We knew them so well that we were regarded as part of the harvest. These were the days of the horse-drawn binder and the three Suffolk Punch that drew the binder were already at work.

A wide swathe round the outside edge of the corn had already been scythed so the binder had a clear run. As the corn was cut, the machine bound it into sheaves with binder twine. Men following the binder would collect the sheaves and build them into shocks, standing them base down, balanced against each other so that the grain could start drying out and any rain would run off. Later, they would be taken to the farm, threshed, the now-dry grain stored away and the straw made into stacks. Today, all the threshing is done by machine as the corn is cut and the straw packed into great bundles, to be taken away later. No longer do we see the beautiful art of the stack builder or hear the sound of the threshing machine, which told us Autumn was nearly here.

Our great interest was in the rabbits that came out of the corn as the field got smaller and fled for safety into the next field. We each had a strong stick and meant to catch one if we could.

I don't think we ever did, for a rabbit is very fast over the first 50 yards. Even if we caught up with one, I don't think any of us had the heart to kill it.

I remember my brother chasing one to the edge of a field. They disappeared through a gate and come back again farther down the field with the same distance between them – and both were walking!

The farm labourers never seemed to mind us following the binder. Later in the afternoon the farmer arrived with his gun and took up his position along the edge of the corn where he considered most of the rabbits would escape.

When all was over we made our way home, tired, hungry and happy, and if we were lucky with a rabbit from a generous farmer.

Every day was spent like this, though we knew we were coming to the best two weeks' holiday of all – the seaside.

The first years of holidays I remember were all spent in Great Yarmouth. I knew our parents had spent their honeymoon at the Star Hotel by Southtown Bridge and it brought back happy memories for them.

Early in the week before we went, a British Rail van called to collect our large wicker hamper, which contained not only clothes but quantities of food as well. Our landlady would put us up but Mum always supplied the food.

We travelled by train from Bury to Southtown Station. Here, during the holidays, there were boys waiting with handcarts to take your luggage and you walked with them to your lodgings. Ours were in Havelock Road, just back from the front near the Wellington Pier. It was obvious that the parents had known our landlady for a long time.

From then on the holiday followed a definite pattern. After tea and unpacking we walked down to the sea and then along the promenade to the Britannia Pier, admiring the wonderful flowerbeds and seeing what had changed since last year.

At the Pier, there was a large brass weighing machine and you sat in a big brass chair to be weighed. The stallholder recognized us from last year and welcomed us back. The tickets were carefully put away by Mum and, on the last evening of our holiday, we were weighed again on the same machine. Unless we had put on weight then the holiday had not been fully satisfactory. A stroll back along the prom and perhaps a go on one of the hundreds of penny-in-the-slot machines, and we were ready for bed. It had been a tiring day.

Up early on Sunday morning we were ready for another busy day. The baker always left a bag of hot rolls on the front doorstep and there were herrings and kippers for breakfast. Then, as it was Sunday, we donned our best clothes and headed for St. Nicholas Church which was supposed to be the largest parish church in the country.

Dad had sung in a church choir at Bury and still had a pleasant baritone voice. His ex-colleague was in the St. Nicholas choir and always invited him to sing there at the Sunday morning service.

After the service, we set about, what was to us children, the best event of the day. Trams ran from Gorleston to Yarmouth, and then to Caister about a mile up the coast. The great thing was that they were open-topped, which made the journey so much more interesting. They ran on a single track, which turned into a double one so they could pass each other, and there was always the chance that you might meet another tram on a single line with catastrophic results. We caught the tram in Regent Road and then it was off along the coast road to Caister, a small seaside village, which had at least two large holiday camps.

With the River Bure on our left and the sea, the racecourse and the golf course on our right, the journey took about half an hour. Once there, we went down to the beach, had a small lunch, visited the cemetery, which was full of interesting headstones, one of which was huge and commemorated a disastrous shipwreck just off the shore, then it was the tram back to Yarmouth.

We still had one more visit to carry out. Over the river, beyond Southtown Bridge, lived "the Old Aunts". I only knew them by that name and presume they were Dad's relations. He always made a point of visiting them, so down we'd go to the ferry, which was a rowboat taking six passengers. I think the fare was two pence each and the boatman landed us almost opposite the terraced house in which they lived. We made this journey every year and we children never said a word when we got there – just sat and listened to the two old ladies talk to Dad and Mum. They had so much to say after a year's absence but none of it meant much to us.

There are two other things I remember about the visit. A strong smell of paraffin, because they cleaned their wooden furniture with it, and Mum's Sunday hat being blown off into the river on the way back. A strong ebb tide carried it quickly down to the harbour mouth chased by our boatman who cleverly edged it into the bank before it went out to sea. We then had a long hard row back against the tide to our starting point. The five-minute crossing took us half an hour. I think Dad paid him double fare for his trouble – four pence each! Then it was quite a walk back to our digs for the evening meal and an early night.

You could never have a dull holiday at Yarmouth – there were so many things to enjoy. We were quite happy to spend all day on the beach with the friends we made and enjoy the Amusements after our evening meal. The beach was within five minutes walk for us. This brought us down just by the Wellington Pier and not far from the large amusement park.

The same families seemed to come year after year and it was always "See you next year" at the end of the holiday. The grown-ups usually pulled their deck chairs together to have a good talk but they were ready to help build sandcastles, paddle or swim. There was always time for beach cricket and fierce battles were fought between the counties.

We never went back to our digs during the day. It was always possible to obtain a drink or sandwich from the beach vendors who carried their goods in trays and never seemed to tire from their endless walking up and down.

Late afternoon we packed up and went home for the early evening meal. We always washed and changed for whatever the evening would bring.

Both Piers had entertainment to offer. The Britannia had different visiting acts each week and was a bit risqué. We didn't go there very often. The Wellington was our favourite because it had a resident Concert Party which changed its shows every week. This was a real treat for us who never saw a live show at home and only made an occasional visit to the Pictures in Bury for the children's Saturday morning show.

Dad, I told you, who had a good baritone voice, always picked up a new song to sing in the village hall concerts. Strangely, I remember two of them almost word for word:

When the Guards are on Parade

"When the guards are on parade,
In their uniforms arrayed,
Who the blankety, blank said the sergeant
Do you think you are?
This is not the Boys Brigade" etc., etc.

And:

The Carol Singers (to the tune of "Good King Wenceslas")

"In our village Christmas time I says to several mates,
Lookee lads I says, says I, now what about some Waits,
We gets a carol – larns it up,
And on an evening wintry,
We muffles up and sallies forth to try it on the gintry.
Good King Wenceslas looked out we sings with splendid power,
Several neighbours looked out too to see what all the row were,
We sings forte, sounded like a hundred,
Even in the soft bits how we thundered,
Bill our bass, he hurt his face,
We thought that it was torn,
But all agree there were none like we,
To greet the 'appy morn.
'Lah, lah, lah, lah, lah looked out' sings Bill with splendid power,
But still he rather marred it,
Because he never knowed no words, he simply Lah, Lah, Lah'd it.
Then our policeman, old Bob Bates, turns up a' scowling proper,
'Good old Bob', young Percy said, 'at last we've got a Copper'.

Then a change came on the situation,
Bob got nasty and took us to the Station.
'Lookee Bates, we're Christmas Waits' I says to him with scorn.
He says with a sneer 'Well, Wait in here
And greet the 'appy morn'."

Why I remember it so well I don't know. I must have been about 12 years old at the time and I've never heard it since!

By a strange coincidence, while I was writing this, four young men came on the TV and sang that very same song, which I hadn't heard for seventy years!

The Pier also had a very large glass structure where you could roller-skate, and beautiful gardens, which had a different Military Band each week on a bandstand erected in the middle. During the day you hired a deckchair and enjoyed the music. In the evening, things hotted up and everyone danced around the bandstand, finishing with a circle of holidaymakers holding hands, singing and dancing to the music.

The place was crowded at times. My brother, about nine at the time, got lost in the crowd one night. We all went out to try and find him and were really worried when we failed. Suddenly, however, to our great relief, a forlorn little figure appeared with a tear-stained face and the buttons of his coat all done up in the wrong buttonholes. I've never forgotten how he looked.

During the week, on Thursday afternoons, daylight fireworks were launched from the Pier. I've never seen the same ones as them since those days. There would be a 'swish' and a 'bang' and a wonderful paper shape would float down. Every child on the beach raced towards its landing spot to be the lucky one to grab it.

Saturday evenings always ended with a grand firework display over the sea. We were thrilled to bits.

I have one other memory of the entertainment on the Pier, which I have never seen since. The England v Australia Cricket Test Match was being played at the Oval. No television and no wireless meant you didn't get the scores until the next day's newspaper.

When we arrived at the Pier Gardens we found a large green baize board had been set upright at one end. It was obviously magnetised and on it was marked out as a cricket pitch and boundaries. Players and ball were white coloured discs, which could be moved from behind the board.

I suppose that operators sat with telephone headphones on in contact with a commentator at the Oval and moved the pieces as the game went on. You would see the bowlers run up, a small disc move to the batsman and then shoot off across the field while the batsmen took their runs

We sat there enthralled. A boundary was cheered as if we were there and an Australian wicket had us standing up to applaud. One operator, which a sense of humour, would make a batsman start to run after hitting the ball and scurry back when he realized he couldn't make the other end. This always brought roars of laughter. It was surprising that some men sat there all day – much to the disgust of their wives. Never again did I see this being done and I wonder if there is anyone still around who did.

Near the Britannia Pier stood The Aquarium, which held not fish, but a theatre. I was taken to see my first Musical there – "No! No! Nanette", with its hit song "Tea for Two, Two for Tea, Me for You and You for Me" – and fell in love with the leading lady!

Further on was The Hippodrome with its circus. This was one of our greatest treats for the circus floor disappeared under water at the interval, and the second half became a swimming display.

With two cinemas - which we only went to if it rained during the afternoon - and a large amusement park with a Scenic Railway, Yarmouth provided all the entertainment you could ask for.

It must be remembered that it was also a busy port. Timber ships from Scandinavia were always unloading wood on one side of the river and on the other were the fish wharves with the huge trawler fleet with their catches of herring during the season. Standing on the street corners leading to the river the Scotch Fisher Girls filled their barrels with the gutted fish. Every year they came south to do this and were a cheerful crowd who got on well with the locals. Fish was so plentiful that you could see it being loaded into barrels with ice, to be sent to Russia and used as fertilizer.

It was the custom when you were on holiday at Yarmouth to send a box of bloaters home to your friends. A shop on Regent Street specialized in doing this. Packed in a shallow wooden box, they cost very little and usually arrived the day after they were posted. My father loved kippers and cooked them his own way. Put in a shallow pan, boiling water poured over and left for three minutes exactly, then drained and boiling water added for another three minutes. On no account must you boil them in a frying pan and when they are taken out the bones can easily be removed. I still cook my own this way today. They are delicious.

Two steamers carried passengers between Southtown Bridge and Gorleston during the Summer months. They left every hour and met half way down the river. One thing that fascinated me was the small boy – about 14 years old – who was always waiting at Southtown for the ship to leave. As the boat left he would dash over the bridge and run down the Gorleston bank waving from time to time to make sure we knew he was there. He could keep in sight through the timber wharves for half the journey and then ran on the road which is close to the river. When we stopped at Gorleston Quay, there he was with his cap held out for us to give him a tip. I'm sure he did very well. Coppers were welcome in those days and holidaymakers were generous.

I never saw him on the boat returning so I expect he want back on the next boat and then did it all again as long as the trips lasted. He must have been the fittest boy in Yarmouth – and the richest too.

One other place that had to be visited was Yarmouth Market. Noted for its fish-and-chip stalls, it was a buzz of activity. After going there we usually went down a 'row'. The 'rows' were very narrow roads lined each side with small houses and they carried any heavy rainwater down to the river. You could almost shake hands across the street from the bedroom windows.

After a few years, Yarmouth began to get very crowded and our parents decided they wanted a quieter place, so we moved to Gorleston just across the river mouth. We could still enjoy the entertainments of Yarmouth, which was quickly reached by ferry or bus. We found a lady in Bell's

Road who took in two families each Summer – one at the front of her house and the other at the back,

In writing these memoirs, I have noticed time and again how fate can affect one's life. You can plan as much as you like but some small incident can alter everything and you can do nothing about it. You will see what I mean later.

Gorleston was a much quieter seaside resort. Like Yarmouth, it had a beautiful sandy beach and the sea was very shallow even when the tide was in; ideal for young children. Bathing tents were set out in squares on the beach and could be hired for the holiday. One side was open to the sea. Again, the same families seemed to come each year at the same time and we made many friends.

We kept this holiday for the next few years – in fact right up to the time when I left College in 1934 and went to work in London.

Gorleston had its own special attractions. One was a long promenade with cliffs behind, which led to the harbour mouth. Here you walked up the jetty to the Coastguards Office right at the end. Along the beach-side of the jetty were the 'Cosies'. These were a sort of wooden platform which was reached by climbing over a low parapet. Sheltered from the wind, you could lie here and enjoy the beach and the sea and the fishermen with their rods. It was a very cosy place indeed.

At last it was the end of the holiday and we returned home for me to get ready for my new school.

(1) The School and House at Fornham All Saints in 1918

(2) ...and in 2008

(3) Mum, Charles and Dad in WW1 army uniform, 1914

(4) Charlie 1918

(5) Suffolk Punch pulling the binder at harvest time

(6) The beach at Gorleston-on-Sea circa. 1924

(7) Doug and Mollie swept the trophy board at the West Suffolk County School Sports

(8) Yarmouth 1928.
L-R: Uncle Archie, Auntie Mabs, Betty Barnett, Mum, Mollie, Dad,
Douglas, Grandma Loades, Charles, Grandad Barnett

(9) Dad and Mum
out for a walk on the
front at Yarmouth

*(10) The Abbey Gate at Bury St. Edmunds
(Scraperboard by Charles Loades)*

Chapter 6
GRAMMAR SCHOOL DAYS 1925 – 1932

For the first time, I had to wear a school uniform! A navy-blue cap with a yellow band, blazer to match, grey shorts and a stiff Eton collar with tie. These could all be obtained from 'Staffs', a men's outfitters in Bury.

I had never been in the shop before and what attracted me more than my uniform was the way bills were paid. The assistant put the bill and the money into a container, which when he pulled a handle shot off along a wire track and disappeared into the ceiling. A few minutes later it returned with a receipt and any change. This went on all the time from the various counters, a defence against thieves, I presume.

My first day saw me not exactly nervous but wondering what would happen. Unlike today's new pupils, we had not been asked to visit the school before the Term started and meet the Headmaster and Staff.

With Mum's words of wisdom ringing in my ears: "Don't forget to go to Grandma's for lunch" – I cycled to Bury and followed a stream of boys and girls to the school. I found myself in a playground with a mass of other boys, saw a cycle-shed and put my bike away.

Suddenly a bell rang and I lined up with the other new boys. Then it was into the school hall with the other First Year boys and girls. Nobody welcomed us – a teacher read out lists of names and off we went to the two new First Year Classes. Here we met our Form Teacher and registered. The only information I remember was strange: "You will all do Latin the first year and if you are no good at it you will change to Physics!"

I cannot remember how the rest of the day was spent – it was a complete muddle. I did go to my Grandma's for lunch. There were no school meals and I was glad when four o'clock came and I could go home.

But the day was not over yet. In the playground a group of senior 4th Year boys met us and said "Come on, we're going to show you round." That's very kind of them I thought, but I was in for a shock. We were taken into the playground to a shed where we had to bend over a bar and have our bottoms smacked – not very hard, just to let us know that we were nothing. I've noticed this happens in so many societies where new members are put in their place, not by smacking their bottoms but making a new member feel small.

I was quite pleased to get my cycle and ride home. Mum was worried because I was later than expected. Of course she was full of questions and I learnt my first school lesson – tell your parents the good that happened and keep the rest to yourself otherwise they will live in a constant state of worry.

I soon settled into the routine although I must say activities were almost completely concerned with lessons. The pupils came from such a wide area by train, bus, cycle or walking that it was impossible to arrange out of school activities because of travel difficulties. We played our inter-school games mostly during school time, missing normal lessons. A few times we played Saturday mornings.

I realized, when I started teaching myself, just how limited our opportunities were. We never saw the Headmaster except at Assembly or if one was in trouble.

We had no proper physical education lessons. A young member of Staff just took us into the playground and we played handball. I found this a great handicap when I entered College, where many students were skilled at gymnastics – but then, we had no gym!

Our inter-school games – football and cricket - were arranged by a pupil and we were escorted by any Master who happened to be free at that time. Afternoon games were the same – a master was there to keep order but there was no coaching.

Strangely we produced good teams and had a high reputation amongst other schools in the area. This was because we practised by ourselves out of school with some enthusiastic fathers.

This all sounds like a tale of woe. The Staff were competent but the only one I found inspiring was the English Mistress. She certainly helped me and it was my best subject. I found I was naturally quite good at Art – we never had any lessons – and about average at most else. Languages were not my best subject and I changed to Physics at the end of the first year.

Despite my criticism now I was very happy on the whole and made many good friends. But how different it might have been!

My schooldays nearly ended abruptly at the end of the first Term. It was the last week before Christmas and we had a slight fall of snow, which had turned to slush. Cycling was not easy. It was quite dark and I had reached the outskirts of the town when I met a tractor towing a load of tree trunks. This was quite usual in this area where there were many forests.

The tractor had just reached me when a car pulled out from the back, skidded across the road and hit me full on. I came round lying in the middle of the road with someone saying "Is he hurt?" and someone replying "Look at his head". I did not feel much pain and was soon in the West Suffolk Hospital at Bury. I woke up again in the Men's Ward – I was a tall boy – with my head and face in bandages. I spent the whole of Christmas in the hospital recovering from a deep cut on the top of my head, a badly scraped face and another cut on my chin. I was very fortunate to survive and have no permanent noticeable damage except for an inch-long scar on the chin. When people ask me how I got it, I always say, "It's a fencing scar". They are very impressed.

Christmas had not been too bad, with Mum and Dad allowed in for Christmas dinner. Those were the days when the surgeon came and carved the turkey at the end of the ward.

I was able to return to school for the Spring Term with the doctor saying "Don't head a football for a year!" Fortunately I recovered fully, though I sometimes still catch a comb in my four-inch head scar.

As time went on, my brother and sister both joined me at school. On the first day of the Autumn Term, paying pupils would stay after Assembly and go up onto the stage to pay the fees. I paid £3 for myself, £2 for Douglas and £1 for Mollie.

I have always been pleased that I attended a mixed school. I cannot understand why boys and girls should be educated in separate groups and be thrown together at an impressionable age. All sorts of problems arise.

Although we were taught in mixed classes we never had time to form relationships with girls because, as I have said, we were so scattered when we went home. The one girl I would have liked to have met lived 8 miles away and travelled by train to school. Who would cycle 16 miles to see a girl?

It came as a surprise to me in the Summer Term of my fifth year to find I had an important exam to take, GCE, at the end of Term.

Nobody, not even my parents, had mentioned it. Certainly none of the teachers had talked of a syllabus. I always knew I would be a teacher but that would be in 1932, a year away. The exam came and went and I really hadn't experienced much difficulty, except in French. Our teacher, Taffy Jones, was the worst disciplinarian I ever knew and the girls gave him hell in his lessons.

The results were published in the *Daily Telegraph* in the Summer holidays and that day the *Telegraph* replaced our usual *Daily Mirror*. All was well till I came to French. I had failed and I needed a pass for matriculation which would qualify me for Teachers' Training College. What should I do? I was 17 and I couldn't enter College until I was 18 so I could spend another year at school. This seemed such a waste of time for one subject so it was decided I should leave, get a job as a student teacher, have private lessons in French and retake it at Christmas.

I applied for entry to St. Paul's Training College, Cheltenham, and was accepted as long as I passed the French exam.

I left school and was sent to Culford Village School as a student teacher for a year. Culford was about four miles from home so I could cycle there each day. The Head, Miss Pinnock, knew Mum well and she enjoyed having someone else with her. I think I was paid £1 a week and she would often put in a little out of her own pocket.

So I had my first experience of practical teaching.

In the village was Culford Hall, a wonderful building standing in its own grounds of many acres. In front was a beautiful cricket pitch and the owner, an Indian, and a cricketer himself, allowed the village team to play there. As soon as they knew I was at the school they invited me to play for them each week and, as cricket was one of my better sports, I was pleased to accept. We had a wonderful season playing all the local villages, sometimes on the village green, sometimes on these beautiful pitches at the Halls. Elvedon was a great rival as Elvedon Hall was owned by a relative.

Several of us who left school at the same time formed our own football team and called it "The Collegians", as most of us were going to college. We played in a village league. As the goalkeeper, I froze on many a Suffolk pitch during the Winter months.

The other strange thing I did, with three friends, was to form a dance band – again called the "Collegians" and played for dances in the surrounding village halls. Two violinists, a piano, and me on the ukulele. Sounds like a strange combination, but we were very popular and out most Saturday nights. We never thought of charging – perhaps that's what made us so popular!

Where I got a ukulele from I don't know, but I taught myself to play it just the same as so many other youngsters learn the guitar. Nowadays, we might be rich!

When Christmas came, I passed the French examination and was now all set to enter St. Paul's in September.

My brother and sister were still at school, both determined to be teachers. They were excellent at sports and won the Boys' and Girls' School Athletic Championships respectively.

We were great friends with Mr. and Mrs. Quant and their daughters, who lived in the village and had their own grass tennis court. They owned Quant's Shoe Shop in Abbeygate Street in Bury and we spent hours during the Summer playing very often with Dad and Mr Quant. We all became good players – but more of that later.

It would not be right to leave my schooldays without saying something about Bury St. Edmunds, the town where they took place. We were allowed out into the town at lunchtime on condition that we did not meet or speak to any of the girls. I was reported to the Headmaster by a member of Staff for doing this. All I was doing was speaking to a young lady who came to play tennis with us once a week in the evening. I was merely making sure she would be there that evening.

It was the only time I met the Headmaster in his study while I was at School! He said, "Loades, you've been seen by a member of Staff in the town at lunchtime talking to one of the girls, is this correct?" I said, "Yes Sir." He said, "There you are, let this be a lesson to you. She denied it. You see the difference between men and women. Men always tell the truth. Don't do it again!" I never spoke to him again.

Daniel Defoe described Bury St. Edmunds as "A town famed for its pleasant situation and wholesome air, the Montpelier of Suffolk and perhaps of England." Bury's motto is "Shrine of a King, Cradle of the Law" and I must say I love it. For such a small town, it has magnificent buildings and yet with the wide expanses of the Angle Hill - written about by Dickens - and the Market Place, it always seemed spacious.

The Abbey Gate, dominating the Angel Hill, with its gardens and ruins behind. The Town Hall, the Athanaeum, the Corn Exchange, the Cathedral, Moyses Hall and the Theatre Royal are all worth a visit.

The market was always packed with stalls on Wednesdays and Saturdays, and still is. The variety was tremendous from the farmers with their fresh vegetables to the Cockneys who travel from one town to another selling everything. We liked their stalls best of all for the salesman never stopped talking, selling his goods in a kind of reverse auction – e.g. "Here you are Madam, this wonderful saucepan for two pounds – but I am not going to charge you two pounds, I'm not going to charge you thirty shillings – I'm asking one pound with this frying pan thrown in." The trick was to catch him just before he decided to sell something else which meant you really had a bargain.

Those were the days when nothing in Woolworths really did cost more than sixpence, when you could buy a 1000-Mark German bank-note ridiculously cheaply and the Home and Colonial would pat your pound of butter into shape and plant a beautiful pattern on top to finish it off!

To the young man who had lived this country life, College might be a big surprise.

Chapter 7
ST. PAUL'S COLLEGE, CHELTENHAM 1932 – 1934

My friend at the W.S.C.S., Leslie Welham, and I were both fortunate enough to be accepted at St. Paul's. We had no one to advise us on our choice, only the knowledge that some past W.S.C.S. students had gone there.

The only communication from the college was to tell us we had been accepted, the date of the beginning of Term, and to ask us in which subjects we wished to specialize.

We were also informed that we would not be able to leave the College on Sundays unless we wore a hat and white stiff collar. As St. Paul's was a Church College, there would be a short service in the chapel before breakfast each morning. This would also be attended on Sundays by the girls from St. Mary's, our sister college. Otherwise, we would have no contact with the female sex either after the service or in the town. The punishment for breaking this rule would be expulsion.

As I have said elsewhere, in my opinion the practice of keeping males and females separate at school or college was asking for trouble.

We had heard from an old student about the way we could dress. Anything would do for private study, but we should look respectable for lectures, Sundays or going into town. Our college colours were light blue and dark blue, and you had a College scarf, the longer the better. Mum knitted me one about ten feet long. More of that later.

In 1932, attending college or university was a privilege and you would be expected to put up with almost anything to get there, and stay there.

On the opening day, we met at Bury Station to catch the train to Liverpool Street, then the Underground to Paddington, and the train again for the journey to Cheltenham. Neither of us had been on the Underground so that was an adventure in itself.

Leslie lived in Bury and Dad took me to the station on his motorbike. As we said goodbye he inadvertently closed the carriage door on my thumb. Luckily it was only squeezed, but I remember having excruciating pain for several days. A good start!

We managed our change-over without difficulty and the journey to Cheltenham passed without incident. It was when we emerged from the station that we had our first problem. Neither of us had much money – I only had my five shillings-a-week pocket money and some odd coins – so we could not afford a taxi. Nothing for it but to walk, which we did, carrying our heavy cases. We were exhausted when we reached the college main entrance.

St. Paul's looked like a college. Built of Cotswold stone, its three wings formed three sides of a square which contained the Chapel, Gymnasium, and the Dining Hall and lecture rooms with dormitories above. You entered through a very large porch, which had steps leading upstairs, and came to the quadrangle – a grass plot with tennis courts which stretched from front to back. During the week, we were only allowed to use the back gate. On Sundays, we could leave by the front porch resplendent in our trilby hats and stiff collars.

We were met by 2nd year students who took us upstairs to the dormitories. These were in the long wings at the front of the college and consisted of single rooms with one bed and a washbasin. A corridor ran down the centre. We were told to unpack and come downstairs to register. Leslie and I were in different wings and never saw each other again until we met downstairs.

We discovered that, after breakfast and a short return to our bedrooms, we were not allowed upstairs again until after lunch. This visit was only for half an hour and we could not return again till after tea. I presume that this was to keep us away during the time when the girl cleaners were working in our rooms.

All in all, our day went quite smoothly. We made a short visit into the town, were told by the seniors that they would all be returning tomorrow and went to bed tired but content.

A bell woke us in the morning and we knew we had time to shave and dress before going to the Chapel and then to breakfast. Showers and toilets were on a lower floor; no facilities upstairs except for washing. There was a bathroom, if you could find it unoccupied.

The bell told us it was time for the service. The whole programme for the day was controlled by the college bell.

For breakfast we lined up in the corridor to the Dining Hall and sat at the junior table. The seniors had their own. During the day, the seniors began to arrive and by tea-time the tables were full. Nobody seemed to take much notice of us.

Our first morning we woke to banging on the doors and shouts of "All juniors in back quad in P.E. kit." It was 6:30 am and I certainly wasn't feeling very happy. When we were in lines we were told we were going on a pre-breakfast run. Anyone who lived in Cheltenham would stay behind for special P.E.

Then the college cross-country team arrived and off we went. Nobody spoke to us and soon we left the town and were in the country – then we were all alone – all the seniors had disappeared! You can imagine how we felt. It was 7:00 am and breakfast was 7:45 am. If we were not there we'd be in trouble. A quick get- together and we decided which way to go. We would stay together. In the end we arrived back with ten minutes to spare.

We realized then that this was the way we would be treated until the seniors were satisfied we knew our place. I suppose they had a point – several of our year had been Head Boys at their schools and thought of themselves as something special. But I still don't think we all should be treated that way. H.O.P!, (hands out of pockets), was shouted at us across the quad. We had to pass through lines of seniors in the corridor when we went to meals, and though we were never physically assaulted it became very annoying. Some of them really enjoyed insulting others knowing there would be no reaction. I dread to think how they would act as teachers.

The Autumn Term continued this way and at times I was really miserable, but at the back of my mind was always the thought, "You are lucky to be here. Just put up with it!"

We were soon absorbed into the college teams to play surrounding colleges at football and hockey, but as we had no hard courts I was unable to play tennis. We made new friends and although Leslie and I did most things together we had a mutual friend in Eric MacAllister. He was even younger than me and a great sportsman. Our friendship continued for many years, until sadly he died in his early fifties.

Although the end of Term was only a month away, we still had some ordeals to go through to satisfy the seniors.

First, there was the Whitewash Match, which we played in pyjamas. It was a mixture of soccer and rugby and every now and again, injured or not, we were carried off and dowsed with whitewash. Then we ran the whole length of Cheltenham Racecourse. No, we didn't jump the fences!

Finally, there was the Christening, two evenings before the end of Term. We all met in the large porch leading to the quad, and as our names were called out we knelt down by a tin bath and a noxious fluid was poured over us. Some said it contained horse droppings from the racecourse! Then we were given our nickname. Mine was PAN, but when I later asked why, I was told it was nothing to do with my appearance. We escaped to the showers, and when we returned had a pleasant surprise. Our Christening meant that we now enjoyed certain privileges, which were not given to the rest of the juniors. I never asked why we were chosen. One of these was that I could wear my college scarf. I was proud of this, despite the fact it was so long and I was always tripping over it. .

Then it was the end of Term and we were on our way home. The first thing my Mum said to me was "You've lost some weight and what's happened to your hair?"

I never told them what had happened and was just pleased to have survived the first Term.

It was great to be home and we had our usual family Christmas with Uncle Archie and his family, but then, strangely enough, I found myself looking forward to going back for the Spring Term. I had met all my old school friends in Bury and surprised and amused them with my long college scarf – what a sight I must have been – and now there was nothing else to do.

We felt like seasoned travellers on our return trip and the atmosphere at college was quite different. Our period of training was over and the seniors now accepted us as proper students. There were still a few of our year who would always make nuisances of themselves, but they were very much in the minority.

I played goalkeeper for the College 2nd Eleven, and as had happened in Suffolk, froze on the Cotswold village pitches in Winter. I was also able to play hockey, badminton and table tennis.

Life was not all sport, however, and we worked hard at our lectures. My selected subjects had now been sorted out – English, Art, Handicrafts and Geography. Music had been dropped and I had P.E. and Religious Instruction, which we all studied. I was in the Chapel Choir and enjoyed that. It was the only time we saw any girls, but even at choir practice we did not mix. The college was very strict on this and two of our year, one of whom had been a professional footballer, were sent down for dating town girls.

This Term there were none of the silly events of the Autumn Term and we knew we would be doing our first school practice before Easter came. Attached to the college was a secondary school which was known as the "Practice School" and every Friday a class came from there for a lesson with one of our Year. It was held in a circular room with seats in steps round so that everyone could watch the lesson on the floor below. Not all of us had to go through this ordeal, but I happened to be one of those that did. After the lesson, the class was dismissed and the criticism began. I suppose it was useful, but somehow it didn't seem real.

The other school practice took place in schools in Cheltenham and Gloucester. We were given a timetable on subjects we were studying and told to prepare lessons, which our college lecturers would watch. I was sent to Gloucester and quite enjoyed the change of taking a train journey each day.

One sad piece of news was that my Granddad had died. He'd had a full life and enjoyed it, but we would all miss him very much.

Suddenly it was the Easter holiday and I was home again. It was great to see the family, but somehow things seemed to drag. In the short time I had been away I had lost touch with the events at home and I was quite pleased to return for the Summer Term.

For me, this was to be the best time of the year. We had trials for the college tennis six, and I found that all the experience I had had at home stood me in good stead. In fact, in all modesty, I was the best player there, so the college team consisted of five seniors and one junior. We played other colleges from as far away as Wales and local teams on Saturdays and only lost one match all the season. I was proud to be awarded my tennis colours and my name went up on the honours board on the back porch.

I was even more delighted to be elected Captain of tennis for the next year and already looked forward to the Summer of '34.

This was a busy Term. The time flew by and it was the Summer holiday. We said farewell to our seniors and realized that when we returned we would be seniors ourselves, and welcoming a new group of young men. I wondered if they would be treated the same way as we were – somehow I didn't think so.

Our usual Summer holiday at Gorleston was waiting for me and I looked forward to it as much as I always did. My brother and sister seemed to have matured over the last six months and we made as many visits to our friends as we could make together on our cycles. Eric MacAllister came to stay and eventually came away with us to the sea. Time passed so quickly that Autumn Term was upon us before we expected – the last Autumn before, with luck, I would be a qualified teacher.

I had a pleasant surprise when I got to college – I had been made a member of the 'Body'. This was like being made a Prefect at school, but was really more for the organization of the year. There were only 15 of us and we had a room where we met to discuss the day's activities. In the evening, for private study, we were in charge of a classroom – mine was Troy. We called the register and then just stayed to see that no one disturbed the others.

If someone was a continual nuisance we could report him to the Deputy Principal and he would be warned and gated. I cannot remember ever having to do that.

We had our own table for meals and my other responsibility was for laundry, which was collected weekly. Not much of a job, but it would look good on my application for work.

The year passed quickly. The tennis team was undefeated in the Summer and we took our final exams.

It was the custom of Education Authorities to hold interviews at the college for newly-qualified students who would begin teaching in the Autumn. The London County Council (LCC) paid the best salary and I was fortunate to be accepted if I passed my exams. This I did. The Term ended and we said our 'good-byes' and 'see you agains' – which we never did, and then it was back home for the Summer holiday.

I have said before that however much you try to plan your life, fate plays a hand and you are helpless - this is what happened to me.

Chapter 8
A QUALIFIED TEACHER

When I arrived home, everyone was excited and we all looked forward to what might be our last Gorleston holiday together. Douglas had already decided to be a teacher and go to St. Paul's in three years' time – Mollie would follow to St. Mary's two years later.

A letter from the LCC awaited me saying that I was to report to the Education Office at Upton House, Hackney on the first day of the Autumn Term. I had never been to London before except to travel to college and I had no idea where to live. I did know that 'List of First Appointments' meant I could be sent to any school in Hackney regardless of my specialist subjects.

I wrote to the Education Office asking if they could give me the names and addresses of possible landladies. Remember, we had no phone so it was a week before I had a reply. Two addresses sent to me were both at Stamford Hill. I did not know where that was, but presumed it was within easy distance of where I would be working. All I could do was take one of these and hope for the best. This all took time and it was only a week before I was to leave that it was settled – one pound a week including breakfast and evening meals.

In the meantime, we had been to our usual address in Bell's Road for our Summer holiday. This is where fate stepped in. As we got there, another family were just arriving too – mother, father and two girls about my age. Naturally we stopped to introduce ourselves – they were Mr. and Mrs.

Brewer, their daughter Betty and her friend Dorothy. They had been coming for years, as we had, but at a different time so we had never met.

They left for the beach the next morning, just as we did, and we strolled down together. Yes, they were booking a beach tent in the same group as we were and before we knew what was happening we were settled in adjacent tents.

By the end of the morning we knew all about each other. They came from Edgware in North London. Betty and her friend were about my age and the former was a secretary at Unilever. Dorothy unfortunately was not very well.

They stayed on the beach all day, as we did, and we all walked home together. I don't know whether it was because I had been starved of female company over the last two years or not, but I felt a strong attraction to Betty immediately and she seemed quite happy being with me.

Our holiday continued in the same way as usual, beach during the day and visits to Yarmouth in the evening. The two families seemed more and more drawn together. They were very interested in the news that I would be going to London in September.

By the second week, Betty and I were alone quite often, much to the amusement of my brother and sister. Finally, on the last night I suggested we go down to the end of the Pier to see the moon rise across the sea. All the others seemed to have something else to do so we went by ourselves.

I talked about my going to London and told her of my apprehensions in going by myself to a strange place and my first job. She sympathised and said, "Don't worry, give me a telephone call and you'll know you're not alone."

We were the only people on the Pier as the moon rose, and I put my arms around her and kissed her. I immediately apologized and she said, "Don't apologize – do it again!" For the first time I knew I was in love!

The next day we all went home and Betty's mother said, "We shall be pleased to see you when you come to London" and I felt that at least I wouldn't be completely alone.

The last week of the holiday passed quickly as I tried to gather all the things I needed together. I travelled on the Sunday to give me a free day to get my bearings before I reported on the Tuesday. Somehow this seemed a much more final departure than before and it was the only time I ever saw Mum in tears.

The journey was uneventful. Being a Sunday, London was quiet and I caught a bus to Stamford Hill and found my lodgings quite easily. I knew the Bernstein's were Jewish but that was about as much as I did know about them. The husband, Frank, was away for long periods and I never got to know him well. They had two daughters, one married and living away, while the younger one was still at home although working nearby. There was one other lodger, a commercial traveller of whom I saw little as he was out early and home late. My room seemed quite adequate and I understood I could use the lounge downstairs if I wished to. The evening meal was taken with the family and we soon learned a lot about each other.

On the Monday, I decided to find my way to the Education Office where I had to be the next day, which I did quite easily. I bought a map of the district and walked back.

I spent the Monday afternoon 'organizing' myself for Tuesday morning. I wrote letters to home and to Betty just to let them know all was well, and wondered what the next day would bring.

Actually I don't remember exactly what did happen at the Education Office. I saw an officer who told me that a school near Dalston had a master absent until Half-Term and I would take his place. There was no mention of subjects; just a letter for the Headmaster.

The building was like all LCC schools. It had three floors – the ground floor for infants and primary pupils, the first floor for secondary girls and the top floor for secondary boys. There were very few mixed schools in the LCC in those days. The playground was overlooked by a six-story hospital.

I went in and up the stairs to the top floor. Nobody stopped me to question who I was. The Headmaster's room was marked, so I knocked on the door and went in and handed my letter to the man behind the desk. There was not a word of greeting, just, "Oh, good, Mr Lewis is away until Half-Term. I'll take you along to his 3rd Year Class." We went to the Form Room and found the class with a teacher who was obviously standing in for Mr. Lewis. He seemed pleased to get away. The Head said to the class, "This is Mr. Loades. He will be with you until Half-Term," and then to me, "The Register is in the desk," and left. No Timetable, no syllabus, nothing else!

The room was a typical LCC classroom of the time – large, with the desks rising on steps to the back of the room and a teacher's desk facing the class.

Those were the days when there were no Heads of Departments and the classes stayed in the same room all the time – only going into the hall for P.E. and Assembly.

I suppose they let me off lightly the first day, though they could see I was a young teacher new to the job. I asked them about the timetable and they said there was one in the desk – and there was. So we got through the day by me giving out the appropriate text books and reading them through with them. I can't say it was very inspiring and I was determined to do better tomorrow.

I asked a few boys to stay with me after school to go through the cupboards, in the hope I might find some suitable books for tomorrow. They seemed rather surprised that anyone would want to stay after the school bell had gone. I asked them about games – they didn't seem to have them. There were no out-of-school activities and I already realized just how bored with school they were.

It is curious, but I don't remember any of the Staff at that school or even going into the Staff Room.

I took the textbooks for the next day's work home with me, so that at least I had something to teach. My landlady asked me how I had got on and I said "alright," and that was about it.

I can not say that I went happily to school the next morning but this was my job; I did not know any other, and I had to make the best of it. I said, "Good Morning" to the class and they seemed surprised at that. I called the register and found several pupils missing, and nobody knew why.

The lessons didn't go too badly although the children were woefully short of general knowledge and many of them had difficulties reading.

School dinners (i.e. lunches) were not provided at every school in those days, but the poorer parents could apply and they were made available at one of the schools in the district, which they had to travel to. Having a school dinner provided was considered as something of a stigma, and many parents would not apply for them so the pupils brought sandwiches and ate them in the playground. This meant a large numbers of pupils having nothing to do for an hour at midday, leading to trouble, because they could not stay in the building and were completely unsupervised.

I was fed up with lunchtimes too by the end of the week, so on the Friday afternoon I said, "Next week I'm coming into the playground at lunchtime. If you've got footballs or cricket bats and soft balls, bring them with you and we'll see what we can do."

I phoned Betty on the Thursday evening and told her a bit about my experiences, though not about the worst ones. She agreed to meet me outside Oxford Street tube station at 3 o'clock on the Saturday, at a Lyons Corner House. There were many of these restaurants in London with their famous 'Nippies' waitresses. She told me that she had been waiting for a call and looked forward to it. She also told me the sad news that Dorothy, her friend, had tuberculosis and was in the hospital, so she was very lonely.

I found that Camden Town was my nearest Tube Station for the West End. It was also on the Edgware-Morden Line so we could travel back together as far as that.

Naturally I got there early. I waited and waited, and waited, and no Betty. Mobile phones had not been invented, so there was no quick way to find out what had happened. In the end, I thought she had decided not to come and the only thing to do was go home. I walked round the corner onto Oxford Street and there she was! I had been at the Tottenham Court Road entrance and she at the Oxford Street entrance. We were both so relieved. What would have happened if I had gone back through the Tottenham Court Road entrance? I've noted before how fickle is fate - and here was another example.

We spent the evening just walking and talking. One of the disadvantages of being a teacher is that you get paid at the end of the month. That would be in another three weeks so I was still depending on my parents. It didn't seem to matter though; we were so happy together and the last week seemed only a nasty dream. We parted at Camden Town already looking forward to the next Saturday.

Back at school on the Monday, I went down to the playground at lunchtime and found a lot of the boys with footballs and cricket bats – not all from my class. By the way, we still hadn't had an Assembly, and I'd only met other Staff in the corridors, but no-one had stopped to speak to me.

I split the boys into groups and got them going. It was all rough-and-ready but they soon settled down to organize their own games. I joined a cricket group and they persuaded me to bat. When I hit my third ball through a second floor window of the hospital, I could feel I had gone up in their estimation. Luckily it was a tennis ball, and a smiling nurse appeared at the window to throw it back to us. From then on, I think most of the boys considered lunchtime the best time of day.

Keeping the Register seemed to be the most important job of all. It was called every morning and afternoon and then, on Friday afternoon, totalled up and sent to the Head. If totals didn't agree, you were in serious trouble. I don't know why such importance was given to this, for it was quite easy to mark someone present when they were away and nobody would know.

The job had to be done, with forty boys waiting for a lesson. To get over this I devised a number of quizzes for the first period, and for the second I read out loud to the class. I gave a small bag of sweets as a prize for the quiz competitions and found that they worked away quietly, so I could do the work that I had to do.

For my readings, I chose books which had a sense of adventure in their stories. *Tom Brown's Schooldays* and *Tom Sawyer* were favourites, and one boy said to me when I left at Half-Term, "We shall miss your reading Sir," which was some repayment for the trouble I'd taken.

However, I did not think this was the kind of teaching I wanted, and I was quite pleased when Half-Term came along.

Betty and I had seen each other every weekend. We knew the streets of Inner-London very well. We had been to the cinema once or twice, but the best had been when I was invited to hers for a whole Saturday and stayed for an evening meal before returning to my lodgings.

When Half-Term came, I thought that I would go back to Suffolk for the week. Mum wanted to hear how things were going at school and I needed a change from living in lodgings. Betty came to see me off at Liverpool Street Station on the Saturday, and I promised to write – we still had no telephone, but I would be back on the Tuesday.

I had already been told I would be at two schools when I returned – one in the morning and a different one in the afternoons. I looked forward to the change.

After the Half-Term it was back to my new schools. They were much better organized than the first one and life was much easier, although I was still not teaching my specialist subjects. I was accepted on the staffs but I knew I should be moving again after Christmas so there was really not much purpose behind it all.

I still met Betty every weekend and had also got to know her cousins, two ladies who were both teachers and lived with their parents in a very large house whose garden ran down to the river by Putney Bridge.

Her Aunt Ada had taught in Gorleston all her life and was now living there on the seafront in a house she had built when she retired. With her lived an old friend, Billie, also retired, who had been a secretary to a stockbroker at the London Stock Exchange. He had a family somewhere but that remained a mystery. In those days these things were not talked about. He had a car as well, and they came to London quite often.

It was a strange relationship. Ada had real character and a mind of her own and was loved by Betty and her family, who I'm sure did not agree with her way of life. They were known as Auntie Ada and Uncle Billie and we got on well together.

Christmas came, and with it a problem. As Betty was still working she only had three days holiday, while I had two weeks. The idea of one of us going to the others for the actual Christmas holiday was out of the question so we both spent the time with our respective parents and made the best of it that we could.

My new school was Berkshire Road. It was further away than the others, backing onto Hackney Marshes and Eton Manor playing fields.

I could feel this was a good school the moment I walked in. The Headmaster, Mr. Widdecombe, even got up from his chair to shake hands. He was in his late fifties and full of enthusiasm for his work. There was a sense of urgency. He smoked a pipe so furiously that one side of the bowl was burnt away and he was always brushing off burning pieces of tobacco.

He took time to find out what I had been doing so far, what my background was and which subjects I really liked teaching. Finally he said, "I shall have a vacancy here in the Autumn, and when you've spent a couple of terms teaching what you want to teach we'll have another talk." I sensed the same approach in the Staff Room. There was a good mixture of teachers of all ages. I felt it was up to me now – here was a chance to settle down.

The school was a bit farther away, and as well as a bus ride I had a train ride to Victoria Park Station, and a walk after that.

Now I was much happier and I was made even more so by Betty's mother saying, "You're over here so much we've got a spare room, come and stay the Saturday nights and go back on Sunday." We were both delighted with this – now we could do so much more with our extra time.

I would not want you to think that I was unhappy at Stamford Hill. Mary Goldstein looked after me extremely well and I'm sure she understood the situation.

At school, I now had the chance to take some art lessons and buy the materials I needed. I still taught the basic subjects but to these I added games. This was a real bonus and it helped with my relationship with the boys. We played our games in the school league at lunchtime, having to miss the last lesson of the morning if we were playing away from home.

There was great rivalry between the schools and often we had two or three hundred adults lining the pitch who were fervent supporters, and let you know it. After I heard the story of the referee who shook his finger at a particularly noisy father and had it grabbed and broken, I decided to qualify as a Referee. At least I could show my qualification if my finger was grabbed! Seriously though, the matches were played hard but fairly. The season ended with the knockout final being played on the pitch of Leyton Orient FC. All the boys schools closed for the afternoon. Admission was one penny.

While my teaching life was improving all the time, my relationship with Betty was now very close and I hated seeing her only once a week. It came as a wonderful surprise when her mother said, "Look, you're spending so much of your weekend here, would you like to move into the spare bedroom and come and live with us?" I don't know if Betty persuaded her mother to do this or how it came about, but I knew that we were going to marry some time, and said, "Yes please." No one seemed to be surprised and I somehow knew my life was changing radically and a happy future lay before me.

I was to move in for the Autumn Term and things looked even better when the Head said, "I have a vacancy in the Autumn for a Metalwork teacher with Art, Games and English. It's yours if you want it." Did I want it! I was so happy both at school and at home that I couldn't believe my good fortune.

I must mention again the matter of me going to live at 11 Hazel Gardens, Edgware. Though we took it for granted, I'm sure there were many who questioned the wisdom. So much trust was given to us, but we never thought of betraying that trust.

When the Summer holidays came, Betty had a fortnight off work. Her friend was very ill indeed and could not come home. My 21st birthday was on the 20th of August and we all wanted to be together for that at Gorleston. In the end, Betty's mother and father, Jessie and William, stayed in the house with Ada, and Betty came with us. Somehow we had an even better holiday than usual. I wonder why?

Then it was back for the Autumn Term. I now had a longer journey to make to school, and I was up at 6:30 am every day. Betty would come down early to make my breakfast and then I was off to Edgware Station to get a workman's ticket. At 8 am precisely, a London Transport official joined the queue and if you were behind him you paid the full fare. This made a tremendous difference because the cheap price was only one shilling return. I changed at Camden Town and arrived at Victoria Park for the walk to school to get me there by 9 am. The morning trip was no problem, but if I stayed on for any time after school it meant I would not get home until 7 pm at the earliest, having travelled in a very crowded train. It was a great pity because Victoria Park had a fine athletics track, which we could use. But, after getting home one evening at 8:30 pm I had to give it up.

Life was very pleasant. We were engaged in the Summer of 1936 and it was almost like being married – except we had separate bedrooms. Both families managed to meet during the year and we all got on so well that it was no surprise when we decided to get married in the Summer of 1938. We had saved enough to take a mortgage on a new house in Canon's Park – a short distance away from Hazel Gardens. I was going to make a slightly longer journey to school and Betty would give up her job at Unilever to become a housewife. This was quite the usual thing then. People were even critical of young wives who went on working once they were married. "He can't afford to keep her" was the usual comment.

During all this time, some radical changes had taken place at the school. Mr Widdecombe was to retire in 1938. I have said that most LCC schools were single-sex schools. They decided that we should combine with the girls school below and a Headmistress was to be appointed. This news caused dismay among the Boys Staff for at least eight of them were members of the National Association of Teachers (NAT), which was entirely male and would not work under a woman. I was in the National

Union of Teachers (NUT), which was a mixed union and the situation didn't arise. All NAT members resigned, a Miss Spender was appointed Head and the two schools would become one in the Autumn Term of 1938.

Although I lost some good friends, this change did not worry me unduly as I was still young and inexperienced. The fact that I was about to marry took up most of my thoughts.

Actually, Miss Spender turned out to be very competent and a charming lady. She was the aunt of Stephen Spender, the poet, and very experienced. I was happy with my new timetable and looking forward to the new Term.

We were married at Edgware Parish Church two days after the Term finished. All our friends and relations were there and Betty looked beautiful in her wedding dress. My brother, Douglas, was Best Man and it really was a happy day. We went to Bruges for a one-week honeymoon, travelling by boat, which was a new experience for both of us. It was a wonderful week. Back we returned to our home and enjoyed settling in with our new furniture and garden. We both loved gardening and there was plenty to do. Little did we know what the next year had in store for us, and how dramatically our lives would change.

My brother was in his last year at St. Paul's and I knew he would try for a job back in Suffolk. My sister was in her last year at school and would be going in the other direction to St. Mary's College, Cheltenham, so the future seemed nicely settled.

The New Year passed uneventfully. All my family came up for Christmas and stayed in the two homes in Edgware and Canon's Park, spending Christmas Day at ours. Now that Betty was not working we could both take the longer school holidays. This we did at Easter. The Grey-Green Coaches from King's Cross were very convenient for the East Coast – better than the train. The new school was going smoothly and we were finding a mixed school had many advantages.

As the Summer holidays arrived, we had an invitation from Billie and Ada to join them on their boat on the Norfolk Broads, and we were pleased to accept. It would be the first Summer holiday I had spent away from my family.

All Summer, the news from Europe was worrying, with Hitler threatening to invade Germany's neighbours. We saw preparations for war going on in London – air-raid shelters being built and gas-masks issued. I don't think we really believed anything would happen, although we knew there were plans to evacuate children from London if necessary.

We started our boating holiday about the middle of August and enjoyed the peace and quiet of the Broadland waterways. The motor cruiser was a comfortable one and we toured a different Broad each day. At night we found a mooring and listened to the wireless. I fished a bit and did some painting, and when necessary we all went ashore to buy food. We were at peace with the world.

We were in our second week, listening to the breakfast news, when the shock news came that Germany had invaded Poland – all teachers were to return to their schools in two days' time to prepare for evacuation. This really was quite a bombshell. We immediately made for our berth, caught the first coach home and I duly reported to school. We were told we would be evacuated in two days' time. Nobody knew where we were going, or how many children would be with us. If any wives wished to go with their husbands, they could go as helpers. No mention of husbands going with wives.

We went home really shaken by this. Our new house had to be left – although Betty's mother and father could keep an eye on it. As we were leaving very early in the morning, one of our friends offered us a bed overnight to save us an awkward journey. Each pupil was given a gas-mask, in its cardboard case, and a luggage label with their name and address to tie onto their coats. Parents could see their children onto the train but could not travel with them. Where were we going? That was a secret. I wondered if it might be Fornham All Saints in Suffolk?

Everything went smoothly next morning. Our friends made us sandwiches and I even remember they used Marmite, which I hate.

The station platform was filled with weeping parents and children, and we were seen off by a well-known Member of Parliament. The train headed north and we changed to a steam train at Watford. Still, no-one could guess its destination, but it certainly was not to the East.

Finally after an hour's ride, we drew into a station, whose name had been obliterated in case invading paratroopers should know where they were. Then, at last came the message – we were at Northampton! I don't think it mattered to the children, but most of the adults were disappointed. We had hoped for a small country town or village. Surely Northampton might be a target for bombers, especially as it had a barracks.

The prospective foster parents were waiting with staff from the Education Office and we all had a quick meal together. Everything was very pleasant and our evacuees seemed quite relaxed. But what happened when pairing up began. I thought it was very sensible for the choice to be made by the staff otherwise some children would be left till last and feel they weren't wanted by anybody.

The foster parents were to be paid by the government five shillings a week, which at that time seemed reasonable. The pairings took place and we arranged to meet the pupils at 9 am in a local hall which was set aside for all our needs. At the moment it was a great adventure and going well since many of the pupils had never been away from home before.

Then it was our turn. Betty and I, with a single master, Geoffrey King, and another master and his wife, Mr. and Mrs. Crisp, were taken to an address quite near. It was a large three-story house with a basement that contained a kitchen, sitting room and bedroom. A Mrs. Hervouet and her daughter lived there. The lady was French, a widow, and spoke perfect English. Her daughter was a concert pianist and away for long periods performing.

The mother and daughter lived in the basement and we had a sitting room and three bedrooms. The only snag was the kitchen, which our wives had to use as well. This was never a real problem.

Wally Crisp was an excellent and experienced teacher, as I knew, and of course I was still comparatively inexperienced. Geoffrey King was an older man who had problems with discipline but was a very kind man. Our wives got on well together. They would help by taking children to hospital when necessary and visiting foster homes to see how things were going.

Our bedroom was roomy and comfortable. The one strange thing about it was that when you lay in bed looking at the ceiling you saw that it was painted with a nest in each corner. In three of the nests were cherubs, two males and one female. We learned later that the original owner was a Mr. Wren, owner of the business making shoe polish, which was famous nationwide. Evidently, as each Wren child was born, it was painted into one of the nests. The shoe polish connection was no surprise because Northampton was known for being the centre of the boot and shoe making industry.

The next morning, we met the children in Nelson Hall, a large building which stood on what had been a racecourse in the centre of the town. The course had not been used for racing for many years and now had cricket and football pitches, which were used every Saturday.

All turned up on time and we learned that where we had a reasonable number of pupils we would be given a classroom in the nearest school and teach our own children. We could start that day. The Hall was for our use in the evenings to give some relief to the foster parents.

We had brought a certain amount of equipment – paper, books, etc. - with us, so there was no problem there. We met after lunch and visited our new school, which was quite near. There were other members of senior Staff with us and they were to organise our lessons with the local school. I noticed an air of "Nothing's happening – I'm going home if I can" amongst older Staff, and several pupils said their parents were coming down at the weekend to take them back.

It was certainly a strange time for everyone and made worse when Neville Chamberlain, the Prime Minister, announced that Hitler had been given a short time to withdraw his troops from Poland or war would be declared.

Still nothing happened and I was sitting, a few days later, listening to the wireless when Chamberlain told us we were at war. Somehow I think we expected hostilities to begin immediately but the only thing that happened was that an air-raid alarm went off when a private plane flew over the Channel.

The next weekend, half our pupils went back to London with many Staff. Miss Spender had already been recalled by the LCC and we found that our small group of teachers, three of us, were the only ones left from our party. There were not enough pupils left to make our own classes so we were absorbed by and worked with a local school, and the Headmaster took us over.

I think we would have liked to return home as the "cold-war" continued, but we felt a duty to the children. By then we had let our house. Ada and Billie were asked to leave Gorleston because of the danger of invasion – the beaches all along the East coast were mined. They went inland to a small village in Suffolk, called Coton. With the possibility of the imminent bombing of London, Betty's parents joined them in Cotton, where they all stayed for the rest of the war.

I cannot say it was unpleasant in Northampton. The local teachers were very friendly and we often met out of school. The blackout was a nuisance, as was the rationing, but nothing more. We heard about the Maginot and Ziegfried defence lines between France and Germany and were told by Bud Flannagan in his popular song that we were going to "hang out the washing on the Ziegfried Line". We knew that our troops had moved into France and we were fire-watching at night in the school with a bucket of water and a hand pump to extinguish fire bombs. We saw the Territorial Army ("Dad's Army") being recruited in case of invasion and we carried on with our normal life as well as we could.

Then everything blew up! The bombing of London and other towns started and the 'Maginot Line' proved a useless defence as the Germans poured into France. Our troops, with huge casualties, were driven back to Dunkirk, to be evacuated from the beaches. We were outnumbered in machines and men and all we could do was prepare to resist invasion.

In all this, Northampton remained very quiet. No planes, no bombs. Even the 'Flying Bombs' failed to reach us although we did hear one well outside the town and waited in trepidation for this engine to stop and the explosion to follow. It came down in open country and did no damage.

I was finding things very difficult at that time. There I was, twenty-five years old, fit and well, and yet doing nothing to help the war effort. Dunkirk had been a disaster and we needed every able-bodied man. I felt rather embarrassed when I was on a bus and everyone else was at least twenty years older than me! So I was relieved when I received my 'call-up' papers and asked to go for a medical at the barracks. Although Betty was worried she realized it had to happen and she would go to Suffolk to be with her parents.

I sailed though the medical until it came to my feet. The doctor said, "You have hammer toes – one on each foot." I said, "Yes, I know, I was born with them." "You can't wear army boots", he said. "They haven't troubled me for years." I replied. "I'm sorry", he said, "but I have to fail you." "Can't I join the RAF," I asked. "You wear boots in the RAF." he said, "I see you're a teacher. You are badly needed as such nowadays. Go back home and look after your pupils."

I felt quite ashamed and when I got home wrote to the Ministry offering to go to a munitions factory.

They would not have me, so back to teaching I went.

Wally Crisp, as I have said, was an excellent teacher – he was also a rabid Communist. However he never expressed his views to us but we knew how keen he was. When Russia supported Germany after the first year of the war he was devastated. Within a few months he died. We all thought it was of a broken heart.

This left me, at twenty-five, as the most senior Master remaining! I was quite happy dealing with the small number of children left with me at the Bective School. I always did like organizing!

As Christmas of 1939 drew close, we realized that we would be spending it at Northampton. My brother left college and had been 'called up' immediately. He was at the barracks at Bury for training. My sister was still at St. Mary's, which had been evacuated to Wales. She would spend Christmas there.

On the last Saturday of the Christmas Term, I received a letter from my father. As I read it I thought it was very strange and then I realized it was not meant for me, but my sister. He said he was very worried about Mum, who had been ill for a week. Could she come home for Christmas to help look after her? His tone was so desperate that I decided to go down myself the next day – the Sunday. There was one train from Northampton there, and one back in the evening. I could not let him know I was coming.

Off I went and arrived at Bury in the early afternoon. It had been snowing and there was no transport from the station. The one porter couldn't help me so there was nothing to do but walk the two miles. I found myself ploughing through snow up to my knees at times but reached the house and rang the bell. Dad's face was a picture of amazement and relief when he opened the door. I explained to him why I had come and he took me upstairs. He said the doctor had come once and had said she had influenza. Getting a doctor out from Bury in this weather was a marvel in itself.

I could see it was pneumonia. She was light-headed, very hot, did not recognize me and was talking gibberish. There was nothing I could do and though he was pleased I had come, he realized that it would be the next day before he could get help.

It was getting dark and I had to walk back to the station to get my train. He promised to send a telegram in the morning.

I got back very late indeed and very worried. In the morning, the telegram came to say Mum had passed away during the night. This was a tremendous shock to me. Although I had seen that she was very ill, I had never expected this.

We went home to the school in Fornham immediately. The Christmas holiday had started so it was closed, but people from the village arrived as they heard the news. There were several evacuees there with their foster parents but there was nothing they could do.

Dad was in a state of shock but we had to arrange the funeral before Christmas and Mum was buried in the family grave in Fornham Cemetary. A telegram to Mollie asked her not to make the long and difficult journey home and she agreed to stay where she was.

The whole thing, even now, seems like a bad dream. The most poignant moment was when Douglas, in uniform, stepped forward to salute the coffin as it was lowered into the grave.

Dad agreed to stay with his brother and sister-in-law in Bury over Christmas and we went back to Northampton to look after the evacuees. I don't remember a thing about it. All I knew was that Dad would have to move in the near future, as the new Headmaster, when appointed, would take over the house.

We did go down again in the New Year and helped him go to his brother till things could be sorted out. As far as I know the school closed down and was never opened again. I heard that it had been changed into a private house.

Dad was only 49 when this happened and he returned to work at the Free Press living with his brother. A few years later he re-married and was fortunate to return to a happy life. We were all conscious, though, of the fact that Mum was a very special and outstanding mother, and when I visited the village forty years later she was still spoken of with great affection.

While writing this, looking through some old photographs, I have found an appreciation of Mum that appeared in the *Bury Free Press*. It seems to confirm our belief that she was a quite remarkable woman. I felt it was worth repeating here for it shows just how highly she was regarded.

Born in 1885, Mrs. Loades was the daughter of the late P.C. Thomas Barnett, who, for many years was stationed at Shimpling and Hitcham. Mrs. Loades was educated at Hitcham School and served there as a pupil teacher until she gained her teaching certificate. Soon afterwards she was appointed head teacher at Fornham All Saints, where during the last 27 years she had done excellent work. Mrs. Loades was an active member of the Bury St. Edmunds and District Association of the National Union of Teachers, of which she was a past President and at the time of her death was a member of the Committee and also the Benevolent Fund Committee. Mrs. Loades did much work in connection with the National Savings Movement. She was Honorary Treasurer of the Fornham and Westley National Savings Association and Honorary Secretary of the National Savings Club, two separate savings groups in the village. The remarkable figures produced by these local associations had attracted particular notice on several occasions. It had been said that the Savings Movement at Fornham had become part of the village life and this was entirely due to Mrs. Loades' leadership. She had represented the Thingdoe Rural District Saving Committee at the Regional Conference on many occasions.

Ever since the inception of the Parochial Church Council at Fornham, Mrs. Loades had acted as Secretary and her work in this respect had been greatly appreciated. She was also local collector for Fornham and Westley in connection with the West Suffolk Hospital Contributory

Scheme, a task she had fulfilled since the commencement of the scheme. Another position she held was that of local organiser of the West Suffolk Junior Drama Festival. Charitable causes found a willing worker in Mrs. Loades and she was the local collector for the National Institute for the Blind, 'the Waifs and Strays Society' and the 'Blind Babies Society', while she had also given her active support to the Cancer Relief Fund. For several years she was Honorary Treasurer of the Fornham Women's Institute and had organised a series of socials in the village as well as taking Folk Dancing classes and playing the piano for the keep-fit classes. In fact, nothing was too much trouble for Mrs. Loades and her place will be hard to fill.

There were over sixty floral tributes and the village church was full.

1940 saw the war growing in intensity and we were now involved in many things in Northampton. There were still a number of children left and they also were growing up with their foster parents. I always think what a strange life it must have seemed to them with two sets of parents.

Northampton was still quiet, although we heard German planes going over on the night Coventry was bombed, and we heard the explosions and saw the sky alight as the Cathedral was destroyed.

We managed to get away during our long Summer holidays to stay with Betty's family at Cotton. It was a complete rest from our normal life and these breaks we looked forward to. As those who were here then will remember, we lived from day-to-day wondering when the tide would turn in our favour.

We felt that this was not the time to have a family, but in 1943 Geoffrey was born and Betty had a new interest. Her duties with the school children were minimal and she was happy to look after the baby and the house.

Winston Churchill's fighting speeches kept up our spirits when we thought the war would never end, and we looked forward each week to Alistair Cooke's 'Letter from America' on the BBC radio. Suddenly the D-Day landings took place, although we never realized how long it would take to complete the invasion, but the end did eventually come and we could return to London. I don't know how many of the original evacuees were still with us. We felt as if we had been in Northampton all our lives. How difficult would it be to return home, and me to Hackney? We would soon find out.

(11) Yarmouth to Gorleston steamer ferry service, 1929
(Courtesy of Archant - Norfolk)

(12) Scottish fisher girls gutting herring at Lowestoft
(Courtesy of Archant - Norfolk)

(13) West Suffolk County School 1st XI football team, 1929

(14) St. Paul's College Cheltenham, the back quad, 1932

(15) Charles Loades. College colours for tennis, 1932

(16) Berkshire Road School Hackney cricket team, circa. 1936

(17) Courting couple, Betty and Charles 1935

(18) Marriage of Betty Irene Brewer to Charles Thomas Barnett Loades, 1938

(19) Wartime home of the Brewers in Coton in the 1940s

Chapter 9
HOME AGAIN

Our first difficulty presented itself before we even left Northampton. Where were we going to live? We contacted our tenants at Edgware only to find that they had nowhere to go either and would not leave the house until they had found somewhere. In our hurry to let the house, nobody had thought of what would happen when peace came. They refused to go and who could blame them.

Betty's mother and father were still in Suffolk and could stay there as long as they liked. Their Edgware home was also let and there was no likelihood of their tenants leaving either.

Betty's Aunt and Uncle came to our rescue. You will remember that they lived in a very large house beside the river beside Putney Bridge with their three grown-up daughters. I had to get back as quickly as possible to Hackney and continue with my teaching. Putney was not the ideal spot from which to travel to Hackney each day, but 'needs must when the devil drives' and we accepted thankfully.

It was surprising how many people we knew in Northampton and we had a grand get-together when we left - with a touch of sadness.

The Putney relatives were delighted when we arrived and I knew that if we were not careful Geoffrey would be completely spoiled. We needn't have worried though, as they were very sensible and I'm sure he benefited from his time there.

I had been told to go to a Secondary School near Old Street Station. It was still in Hackney. I recalled my experiences from when I first began teaching, and hoped that this time I could cope better. So much for expectations!

I could catch the Underground from Putney Station after a short walk on the path over the Railway Bridge. The journey to Old Street was not too long, but when I came out of the Station I had my first shock. The whole area had been devastated by the bombing during the war. Great mounds of bricks had been there so long they were green with weeds. A deafening noise met me from the workmen trying to bring some order to the chaos with their automatic drills. This must have been one of the worst bombed areas of the City. It seemed that no one could have survived, and what about children going to school?

Surprisingly, when I found it, the school building did not appear in too bad a state. It was just the same as I remembered Berkshire Road when we evacuated.

Life seemed to be repeating itself as I climbed the stairs to the top floor. I knew nobody and no-one knew me. I knocked on a door marked 'Headmaster' and was asked to 'Come in'. The man behind the desk was middle-aged and well dressed in a blue-striped suit. He rose to shake hands and greet me with a "Pleased to see you, Mr. Loades!" I started to say "I'm pleased to be here," when he quickly said, "I must tell you that we've only been open a fortnight and new Staff and pupils are arriving every day. We are short of books and other materials and we really live from day-to-day."

"Here we go again", I thought, "It's just the same as when I started eleven years ago – but at least I have some experience behind me now."

He got up from behind his desk to show me around, and it was then I noticed something that had been worrying me for some time. The shoulders of his smart jacket were speckled with white and, as he rose, more floated down from his hair. He flicked this away with annoyance and I realized that it was dandruff. Whether it was due to nervousness, I don't know, but he had the same trouble all the time I knew him and must have been very embarrassed. We visited all the rooms that were back in use and I was introduced to Staff and pupils. At least there was an air of control about the place. "You are taking over a 3rd Year form. I'll introduce you to them and then leave you to get to know each other. I'm afraid we have no syllabuses yet. Just keep them busy with what you find in the cupboards."

Most of the boys had not been to school for some time and I think were fed up with doing nothing, so they were pleased to help clear out the cupboards and generally tidy up. After that, I called the register, adding new names to it. Then we sat down and talked.

Some of them had been with their parents here all the war. Others had gone away and come back and gone away again. Remember, this had been going on for six years with them never knowing what the next day would bring. What a terrible effect the war had on that generation.

I explained to them that tomorrow we would work out a timetable together using the books we had. Had anyone got a football? If they could bring it in, we could play in the playground, which luckily had been cleared. They really behaved very well and I left relieved that my first day had gone so quietly.

The journey back to Putney seemed a long one and I was very tired when I got home. Of course I had to tell them everything. The two cousins who taught at Wimbledon and had never been evacuated realized how lucky they were.

Despite our disappointment at not living in our own home, life in Putney was very pleasant. Uncle Jack, who was a builder, was back in business again with plenty to do. Geoffrey was of an age when all the ladies were interested in him. Betty and Minnie, of course, liked taking him out, and at weekends Jack would put us in his car and visit local places of interest such as Kew Gardens or Wimbledon Common.

The River Thames at the bottom of the garden, when the tide was in, came up to about six feet from the top of the garden wall – at low tide it was a long way down indeed. There is no other way to describe the water except 'absolutely filthy'. It was full of rubbish – all kinds of wood fallen off barges, dead cats and dogs, and what looked like sewage. It was amazing that only a few years later, it was reported that a salmon was caught in the cleaned-up river. We used a net on a long bamboo rod to haul in many decent planks of wood and this was cut up and used on the open fires. Fuel was in short supply and expensive.

So, the year wore on. We were unable to travel far with a young child, so we did not attempt any holidays. Douglas had married and now had a son, Michael, a little older then Geoffrey. His wife, Lee, was a teacher as well. They lived in Sudbury in Suffolk. My sister Mollie had married a naval officer, Harry Stretch, who also taught in school. She was living in Cumbria.

There had been no sign of the tenants leaving either of our houses in Edgware and I decided to go the Civil Court to try and get possession. It was sympathetic and said they must leave in six months. To me it felt like six years and I was extremely down-hearted. I went back to Putney. There had been a phone call from Betty's parents saying that their tenants were leaving at the end of the week. They would be going back. Would we like to join them? It seemed a miracle.

Everyone was delighted, even the Putney family who had made us so welcome, and we left the next weekend.

It meant my daily journey would be longer again but I was prepared to put up with that. I had been thinking about my future for some time – I was teaching, yes, but I didn't want to go on in this way for the rest of my life. Edgware and the districts around were under the Middlesex Education Authority. It paid the same salary as the LCC and if I could move there, wherever I went would be a shorter journey. I did not wait for a list of vacancies but phoned the Hendon Education Office asking if I could have an interview. I did know that, due to the war, teachers were in short supply. The Chief Education Officer saw me and I told him about my experiences. I explained why I wished to move and he seemed to understand.

"Well we need someone at a local Mixed Secondary Modern to accompany a young lady straight from college, who is going there to teach Music. You, with your experience, will be a great help with her discipline! You will also be teaching your general subjects as well."

I never expected to be offered such a post but nothing of course could have been worse than the conditions I had faced so far, and I accepted immediately.

"Good", he said, "you start in the Autumn Term."

I had a sudden thought, "Where is the school?" I asked.

"Edgware," he said.

I could have dropped through the floor. The school was only ten minutes' walk from home. Once again my life was changed by fate. You can imagine the astonishment of the family when I got home. It seemed as if a great load had been lifted from our shoulders.

At the time, several years before, when the London Underground was extended from Golders Green to the new Edgware, a high proportion of the population of the former was Jewish, many of whom had fled from Germany and its surrounding countries before WWII. Some had moved out to Edgware with the railway, and since then, their families had settled there too, so we already had a large Jewish community. In fact, there were two Synagogues in the area, one of which was said to be the largest in Europe.

A close friend of mine, who was Jewish, had escaped from Austria just as war broke out. He married an English girl and Peter, his son, and our Geoffrey, grew up together as friends. They lived only a few houses away. I also knew that Jewish people were ambitious both for themselves and for their children, which should make them keen pupils in Edgware School.

In fact, I couldn't wait for the Autumn Term to begin!

Chapter 10
EDGWARE SECONDARY SCHOOL 1946

During the Summer holiday, I did actually go down to take a look at the school from the outside. Strange how things have changed. In the 1960s, it was common practice for a new teacher to be invited in advance to visit the school and meet the Staff. Here I was in 1946, on my way to my first day as a teacher at a strange school at the beginning of a new Term without ever having met or seen the Headmaster before.

The school was situated just off Edgware's main street, almost in the centre of the town. It was reached by a footpath and located right next to the Primary School, which itself faced onto the Edgware Road, which to the south led eventually to Marble Arch and the centre of London. The school was on one floor, which is always an advantage, for, in my experience, pupils using staircases can be a noisy affair.

I introduced myself to the Headmaster. He looked to be quite an old man and I wondered what his ideas were about education. I was not surprised when he told me this was his last year before he retired. A senior member of Staff took me to my form room and said we would be having Assembly in ten minutes time.

The pupils were very orderly and, after I had called the register, lined up and took me to the hall. This was all so different from my experiences at previous schools, I could hardly believe it. As I had arrived knowing nothing about this school before, I wondered what was coming next. It was very much a normal Assembly of the fullest kind, a hymn, a reading from the Bible and some notices about the day. No welcoming back to school and no mention of me or the Music Teacher, though both of us were completely new at the school. Then the piano struck up and we all marched out of the hall back to our classrooms.

I must say this was a rather disappointing beginning. I'd not yet been introduced to the rest of the Staff and, so far, no sign of a timetable.

However, things did improve. The Deputy Head was waiting for me with a timetable. She - yes, it was a woman, as expected - introduced me to the class and said she could be available if needed. I would stay with my Form 3 until the afternoon and then start normal lessons.

Not knowing the arrangements for lunch, I had brought sandwiches and ate them in the Staff Room, thus meeting most of the teachers. They seemed very welcoming and I felt quite at home by the end of lunchtime.

The afternoon gave me the opportunity to have a talk with the class. I found that there were about 350 pupils in the school and it seemed a happy place. There was no Woodwork or Domestic Science because there were no specialist rooms. The only place for PE and Music was in the hall. I had not yet read the timetable, but I hoped I could use my enthusiasm for Handicrafts and Sport. I did know that I had the staple subjects – Maths and English - as well, to help with Music.

The afternoon passed pleasantly enough. There were lessons I would have with my class, and I took the opportunity to organize the room and to get to know something about them. We got on well together and I realized that I had not taught in such a school before. Many had parents who travelled up to the City each day, and were keen on their children's education.

By the time we'd finished, I knew I had to have a talk with the Headmaster and I made an appointment to see him the next day, during the lunch hour.

We met in his room. I realized already that I knew the Staff better than I knew him. But Heads are always busy at the beginning of Term. He asked me how I was settling in and I told him I was quite happy but there were certain things I would like to talk over – one of which was my timetable.

"Oh", he said, "I leave that to the Deputy Head. You'll have to see her."

"Yes, but what I wish to do requires your permission. I see I have all of the Games and PE. I'm pleased about that, but I find you have no football teams competing in the local leagues. Have you any objection to this."

"No, we have not had a PE teacher for years."

"I should like to arrange a Sports Day for next Summer and invite the parents to come. I would like to see the County PE Advisor about this."

"I shall not be there – do what you like."

I realized then that here was a man who was only waiting to retire and as long as I did not upset the smooth running of the school, I really could do what I liked.

I thanked him and left to see the Deputy Head. She was a very pleasant person and I realized that she knew what was happening, and was doing her best to keep things running smoothly until a new Headmaster was appointed in the Autumn.

She said, "You'll find we have a very good Staff here with ideas for the future. They are just waiting for the opportunity when the Head retires. You carry on with what you want to do – just keep in touch with me and I will do what I can to help."

I went away feeling much happier and meaning to start putting my plans into action immediately. After all, the Staff knew what was going on. Maybe some would be willing to help with the school teams.

The first person I consulted was the PE Mistress. She told me she already had school netball teams competing in Inter-School Leagues and wanted to introduce hockey and athletics. She had no lady member of Staff to help and would be pleased to cooperate.

It was essential that teams were entered in leagues now, otherwise the season would start without us and we would have another year to wait. I put up a notice explaining what we hoped to do and inviting any boy who was interested to meet me in the playground after school. Two of the male Staff offered to help. We inflated as many footballs as we could find and waited to see what would happen. Sure enough there were a large number of boys there. How do you quickly choose a football team? All I could think of was to give them a chance to kick a moving ball. You can immediately see who has any idea. Those who wanted to be goalkeepers formed a small group themselves for their test.

I went to the other end of the playground to give everyone a chance to kick a rolling ball and then chose about fifteen from each age group for a second go. It was explained to those who failed the first test that it wasn't the end for them – there would be chances to show me what they could do when we had games periods, but we must have teams ready as soon as possible.

The method worked quite well. We only lost our first league match 7-0, but we had made a start and I was sure things would improve now the interest was there. One difficulty was that when we went for games each week I usually had about forty boys to deal with – there were no spare men to help. I soon had several fathers offering to help on Saturday mornings. This was very encouraging, but I had a family to look after and I was already spending a great deal of time outside school hours.

The only way to try to solve our problems was to have evening meetings with interested fathers and boys. I had been told to 'do what I like" so the meeting was called. There was a good response and we decided to have a small committee of boys, fathers and Staff to make the arrangements.

I contacted the PE Advisor and he came to see me. I found him keen to help and at last we were making progress.

I found the music lessons did not require much 'discipline'. The pupils liked learning songs in harmony. The young lady teacher obviously knew her job, she just lacked experience. It was she who suggested we might have a concert one afternoon and invite parents and governors. The rest of the Staff were pleased too. One of the boys played the trumpet very well. He was in a Salvation Army Band, and he could play solo. I accompanied him and all went well until he had a nose-bleed. We had to stop and deal with this. To my surprise, he decided to try again.

You could feel the tension in the hall as he started and the anticipation that it might happen again. All went well, and there was tremendous applause when he finished. It certainly added interest to the afternoon but not the kind we wanted.

By now, nearly at the end of the Autumn Term, things were going smoothly. Certainly life was much more interesting and happier than this time last year. We had another new Master join us at Half-Term. He came from outside London and was looking for somewhere to live. I was telling him of my difficulty with the tenants. The next day he came to see me and said, "You know what you were telling me yesterday about your house? I've got a proposal to put to you. I'll buy the house from you." I started to interrupt saying, "But the tenants won't go." "I don't mind," he said, "I'll go and live there with them – I can do that." "Well, I said, I'll talk it over with my wife."

For some time I had been thinking what we should do when the house became empty. We were very happy and comfortable where we were and Betty's parents could not afford the upkeep if we left. There were four bedrooms and the whole place was roomy with a garden overlooking the Watford Bypass at the back. The road was at least 50 feet lower than us and lined with trees and wide grass verges. We could hardly hear any sound of the traffic.

There was no doubt what the answer would be. All agreed that we should stay where we were.

The deal was sealed in a few weeks. I never enquired how he was getting on. He left for another school a short time later I never saw him again.

With the money from the sale I could now do what I had wanted to do for a long time – buy a motor car. Life would be much easier without having to catch buses and trains. Betty's mother and father were now in their seventies and we could make much longer journeys with Geoffrey.

Not many cars, if any, had been made during the war so it had to be a second-hand one. I settled on an Austin 10, which had been new in the 1940s and seemed in good condition. It would seat five, which was just right for us. Now I had to learn to drive.

I did not realize until later how good the instructor was, due to my lack of experience. We had never had a car in the family. I learned the fundamentals in the first lesson and when he came again he said, "Now I'm going to teach you how to use the gears so well that changing gear will soon be second nature to you." I was a bit dubious about this, and even more so when he said, "We're going to drive up Oxford Street. Get in."

He directed me to the Edgware Road and then it was a straight three-mile run to Marble Arch, with the traffic getting thicker every mile. He treated me as if I was an experienced driver giving quiet words of advice. He certainly gave me confidence and I realized what he meant about gear changing.

We rounded Marble Arch into Oxford Street with a London bus on one side only six inches away, and a lorry on the other. Down Oxford Street we went, turned left at Selfridges and made our way back to Edgware via

Regents Park, Swiss Cottage and Hendon. He was right, I felt I'd been driving for years – although I would not have liked to be on my own.

A few weeks later, I took my test and passed – all due to my tutor. Billie and Ada were back in the house at Gorleston. I knew where we should be going for our first long journey.

Christmas was quiet, with a few friends coming in the evening. It was the first Christmas we had spent at home for eight years.

The Spring Term was uneventful. We saw nothing of the Headmaster – the school was run by the Deputy Headmistress, who was very capable.

The school was now divided into four houses – red, blue, green and yellow for our coming Sports Day. Every pupil would be taking part on the day in Team Games, which we were coaching in PE. The football team won a match, much to everyone's delight, and we looked forward to next year.

The Easter holiday gave us the opportunity to drive to Gorleston to stay. I had not done a long journey yet but felt I could take my time and enjoy it. Sure enough, all went well and we stayed a week. It was nice to be there, despite the fact that there were still some mines to clear from the beach.

Back home we prepared for the Summer Term. Everything ran smoothly. We now had cricket and athletic teams, and I felt that at last on the games side there were opportunities which the pupils had not had before.

Our much anticipated Sports Day drew near. The Headmaster again said he would not be coming. I made sure the PE Advisor would be there. Following afternoon registration, the whole school walked to the playing field. It was about half-a-mile away, so we must have been quite a sight, but buses were out of the question. We arrived to find a very good turnout of parents and got under way. All the Staff knew what to do and had their teams ready. Since everyone was taking part they had to keep in their own groups to be ready for action.

I had been rather concerned over how things would go, but I needn't have worried. There was a lot of enthusiasm and laughter. I don't think the school as a whole had ever done anything all together before – it was great to see the pupils enjoying themselves so much.

Tired but happy, the Staff went back to school for a cup of tea together. One of them said, "I wonder what the Head will have to say in the morning?"

Then fate stepped in again.

We had barely arrived the next day when the Deputy had a call from the Education Officer to say that the Headmaster had collapsed yesterday and died. We were dumbfounded! We were to keep the school open as the pupils were there.

It was a sad moment. I realized how little I knew about the man. I never did know if he had a wife and family. The rest of the Staff were the same. His last year must have been a lonely one.

The Chairman of the Governors came in the afternoon to say that the Deputy Head would be in charge until the end of the Summer Term, when a new Head Teacher would be chosen to start in the Autumn. That gave us all food for thought.

When we broke up for the Summer holiday, I thought how much happier I had been for the last year – to be at home again, to know I would be returning to the same school and to feel that I had been able to organize something myself. Mid-holiday, all the Staff had a letter informing us that a Mr. Middleton had been appointed Headmaster to start in September. A week before we returned, we each received a letter from him personally, saying that he would be at the school on the Monday before the Autumn Term began on the Tuesday, and he would like to meet any Staff who could call in.

I wondered what the rest would think of this. To me it was the right thing to do – so different from what I had experienced before.

Now that we had the car we could go to Gorleston when we wished, and go we did, taking mother and father with us for a fortnight and leaving them there. On the way back, we called on my brother Doug, his wife Lee, and their sons, Michael and Robert, who were now about six and three years old respectively. They were both well and settled in Sudbury, and both teaching, Doug at the Secondary Modern and Lee at the Infants School, which Michael attended.

Then back to Edgware and time to be alone together with Geoffrey – the first time since he was born. He would be going to Edgware Infants School in one year's time, when everything would change again.

I went down to school on the Monday morning. As it happened there were no other members of Staff there yet and I saw Mr. Middleton alone. He seemed pleased to see me and asked a few personal questions before we touched on the subject of school. He was in his late forties, dark and tall. I'm six foot and he was slightly taller. He was well dressed, gave the appearance of being used to being in command and asked me some quite searching questions about my career.

I soon found I was telling him about my experiences both before and after the war and how disappointed I had been with most of my schools in London, and with the last year at Edgware. He asked what I thought a Secondary Modern School should be like and I said that none of my schools had been prepared to widen the timetable to interest and extend the more gifted pupils. Failing to pass the "11-plus" did not mean the end of the world. Given the opportunity, I'm sure some of them could take GCEs by the time they were sixteen and all would benefit from a wider timetable, with contacts with the local Technical and Art Schools. The great thing was to give them something for which they could aim; not for them just to come to school because they had to, but because they wanted to. I had found, in a small way, that even forming a football team had helped, and I knew the Staff felt the same way and would welcome someone who was prepared to lead them in that direction.

Other Staff had arrived by now, and I knew he would want to see each one privately so I excused myself. As I left the room he said, "I'm glad you came. Many of your views I agree with and I think we shall work well together."

As I went home, I thought that at last there was somebody who could develop a school of the kind I'd always imagined, and I looked forward to working with him.

Tuesday morning we all went into Assembly. The Head introduced himself and did not attempt the usual type of Assembly. He had the Staff sitting on the stage, and he sat the pupils down and spoke to them. There were no changes in Staff. School would close earlier in the afternoon so he could hold a Staff Meeting and he hoped they would have a good Term. They left the hall form-by-form in a very orderly manner – without a piano playing them out. A note to each of us had said that we would use last Term's timetable until the end of the week, when we would discuss any changes which might be made.

It would take time to reorganize but when we discussed things in the Staff Room we felt quite hopeful.

The Autumn Term was uneventful as we got to know Mr. Middleton. We did not know much about his home life but we knew he had a wife and family, that he had been an above-average hurdler on the athletics field and that he was an ambitious man. Gradually things began to change. Assemblies became more interesting with the pupils taking an active part. The House System was extended from our first simple one, which we used for Sports Day, to include all aspects of school life, with four of the senior members of Staff being appointed House Tutors.

Much more contact was made with parents, who were encouraged to visit the school for evening meetings. A School Council was in prospect and generally we felt we were part of a family and not ploughing a lone furrow. I thought that being so close to London itself and with such easy access we would use the fact to make visits to some of its famous sights, and we decided to talk it over with our classes and come up with ideas for the Spring Term.

My brother, whom you will remember was living and teaching at Sudbury in Suffolk, had discussed with me the idea of an Exchange Visit for boys between our two schools. The party would have to be boys with two male teachers in charge. Twenty pupils from each school would host the pupils from the other school in their own homes for a week, starting with a week in Sudbury. The Sudbury boys would then return with their Edgware guests, to be hosted by the latter for the second week. We would arrange programmes of local visits to places they would not normally be able to see.

Our respective Headmasters liked the idea and we decided to take 4th Year boys late in the Spring Term when the weather should be at its best and the days becoming longer. We had no trouble getting volunteers and paired the families off at random. We encouraged them to write to each other before the journey so they would not meet as complete strangers.

We had not seen much of Doug's family over the past year, but now I had a car I thought how good it would be if we could arrange for them to come and spend Christmas with us. The boys had always got on well together and it would be a much more interesting Christmas for them. I would drive to Sudbury and pick them up a few days before Christmas Day, then take them back home again whenever they wanted to go.

I had never done a long journey in Winter before. The car had no heater and I found it very cold indeed. We brought hot water bottles back with us on the return journey, which did improve matters considerably.

It had been a long time since we had spent such a Christmas together – since before the War, in fact, and we thoroughly enjoyed it. Little did I know then that we would do the same thing every year for the next twenty-four years – until retired. Doug got a car a few years later, saving me a journey. One year, we had a great party when Mollie, Harry, and their three children, Linda, Peter and Alan, all came as well. I'm not sure where we all slept – most on the floor and in camp beds I think!

Our Christmases were very traditional, but never dull – opening our presents all together, a large turkey for Christmas Lunch, the Christmas Pudding aflame with brandy and containing the hidden silver sixpence, which we hoped no-one would swallow and, of course, the crackers and the hats. I remembered times in our younger days when we couldn't afford a turkey, and a chicken was a great treat! Another large cold meal later and we spent the evening playing all sorts of games and quizzes and generally enjoying ourselves.

Boxing Day was always the same; the men and boys went to a football match in the afternoon, either Arsenal or Tottenham, our nearest First Division clubs, because they played at home every other Christmas. The ladies were thankful for one quiet afternoon after their efforts the previous day, although one year we treated them to a Ballet – the Nutcracker Suite – at the Covent Garden Opera House.

I remember being eager to get back to school that particular year in order to start putting the plans for the Exchange visit, or School Journey, into action.

There was something else I wanted to do in this Spring Term as well. With the Physical Education (PE) Mistress eager to help, there was now a real interest in sport throughout the School, and I wanted our teams to take part in the District Sports, which were to be held in the Summer Term. If they did well there, then the way was open for them to go further still. In those days, Hendon was very proud of two of its "sporting sons", the Compton brothers, Leslie and Denis, who had reached the top playing for England at both cricket and football, so here was something to aim for!

I had noticed the previous Summer at the District Athletics Sports, when all the schools could compete, that one Boys School had stood head and shoulders above the others, and won the trophy easily. It was my first Summer and we had hardly any entries. I was so interested that I took the trouble to go through the results and see in which events they had done well.

The High and Long jumps were held on an evening before the main Sports Day as they took up a lot of time and were difficult for the public to watch. I found that this school had won nearly all the jumps. As there were four age groups in each competition and there were five points for the winner each time, this meant a huge advantage to the winning school.

The other interesting fact was that the same school had won both the hurdle races which were held on the day. What I intended to do was make sure that we had competitors in all the events and start serious training in the Spring Term.

In one way we had an advantage. On the school site, we had a reasonably big area that had not been tarred to use as a playground. It was large enough to have high and long jump pits and also a short run over hurdles. We dug our own jumping pits and filled them with sand. These were the days before the "Fosbury Flop", when the style used for the high jump was a scissor jump. In the latter, you landed on your feet, in the former you land on your back and need a considerable depth of rubber matting to break your fall.

We soon had pupils interested and helping when we told them that we intended to have a big entry in the District Sports. Every lunchtime, when the weather was fine, we coached them. Anybody could take part – we would pick the entrants later.

We managed to get a few hurdles, and here again we soon had enthusiasm when they found that you don't jump hurdles separately but glide over them with the same foot leading at each hurdle, and the same number of paces between the hurdles.

We also worked hard on relay takeovers, making sure that the baton changes were made smoothly, with both runners at full speed. I felt if we did well in these events and reasonably well in the sprints, we stood a good chance of achieving a high position on the day.

Time passed quickly and our Exchange Visit drew near. There had been so much contact between the two parties that there should be no problems at the actual meeting. My mind went back to the war evacuation and I thought again of those children going off, at short notice, to live with strange people in a strange place and not knowing when they would see their parents again.

Everything went smoothly and in just over two hours we arrived at Sudbury. It seemed as if the whole town had turned out when we came to the Market Square, but then I remembered it was a Saturday and a Market Day. All the parents were waiting at the school and took their visitors off home. We would meet again on Monday morning for our trip into Suffolk – meanwhile they could get to know each other better.

Over the weekend we compared programmes and made sure we had all eventualities covered. On Monday we were going to Bury St. Edmunds' and as soon as we were on the coach, off we went. A half-hour's ride brought us to Bury and Angel Hill. We had decided to see the town in the morning and the Abbey Gardens, with its magnificent gate and ruins, in the afternoon. Anyone who got lost was to return to the Angel Hill, where the coach was parked.

Bury is a good town to visit – there are so many things to see. First we went to the Cattle Market which was a place none of the boys had seen before, then to the local paper, the *Bury Free Press*, for a tour of the works where Dad had been all his life. Then it was back to the centre of the town to see some of the finest buildings – Moyes Hall, now a museum, the Corn Exchange, where the farmers used to meet to find buyers for their corn. Then back to Angel Hill to the Athenaeum and the Angel Hotel that Dickens mentions in his books.

We collected our lunches from the coach and went to sit in the Abbey Gardens. It was too early in the year for them to be in their full glory with their massed beds of flowers. After lunch I conducted a tour of the ruins that brought us to mid-afternoon and ready to make our journey home. We made a detour on the way through Fornham to show them where we were born and tell them something of life in the country. When we reached home, we were a tired party and ready for bed.

I have been into some detail with our first excursion because I want you to see that we were determined to make the most of our time.

On the Tuesday, we travelled to a large pottery firm and spent the morning there seeing all types of pottery being made. The Suffolk countryside seemed a strange place to make pottery, but it just happened that a large deposit of suitable clay was found near the site. The journey home took us through several interesting Suffolk villages.

Wednesday was also a Market Day in Sudbury and, as was so typical of these towns, the place was crowded with shoppers from the villages around. The Market Square was packed with stalls of all kinds and it was an education to walk round and listen to the talk – often in the broad Suffolk dialect – 'Where be ye goin' bor?' 'I be goin' down the market' in the slightly sing-song tones of a Suffolk man.

After a school dinner, it was off to Gainsborough's House to see the works of the famous artist. He was born in Sudbury and his statue stands in the Market Square. We purposely didn't try to fill the evenings; we let each household make its own plans.

On Thursday we were shown round the school in the morning and after lunch played football against them. We were somewhat of a motley team – I couldn't guarantee eleven good footballers in my party, but it was good fun.

Friday, our last day, was rather special, as we were going to Flatford Mill – made famous by Constable's painting *The Hay Wain*. The country really is beautiful round there and we spent a pleasant day by the river. Once we had seen Willy Lotts cottage we went for a long walk. It was surprising how little the town boys knew about the real countryside and we enjoyed enlightening them.

In the evening, parents and boys met us in the school and we all agreed that the first week had been a great success.

The next morning it was back to Edgware by train to be met by the parents of our boys. Most of them had been in touch by phone during the week, so they knew everything was going well.

Once again, we were to meet on Monday at school. Things were slightly different here because our pupils were scattered over quite a large area. In the end, we didn't have any problems. Just to travel on the Underground was a new experience for the Suffolk boys, and we used it instead of the coach every time we went up to "Town".

We did the normal sightseeing – the Tower of London, HMS Belfast, the Houses of Parliament, where our two MPs showed us round. Perhaps the most exciting was our trip to Heathrow and onto the viewing platform to see the planes land and take off. In those days, flying was still a huge adventure for most people. A final Coach Tour all around London, including Trafalgar Square and Buckingham Palace, saw us all tired but very happy.

We had enjoyed ourselves and made new friends. I saw one of my boys twenty years later and he said he was still in touch with the family he had stayed with. The local newspapers loved it. "Brothers on Exchange Visit" made it sound as if we had been to the ends of the earth! Still, it was good publicity for the school.

Once back, the Easter holidays seemed to be immediately upon us. This one we spent at home. I was looking forward to the Summer Term, to the Sports Meeting that would prove whether our coaching had been worth it. I would not want you to feel that the school revolved around me and my doings. There was no doubt that our Headmaster was having a lot of effect on the general progress – new courses were being planned for next year, which would give a wider choice of subjects to the older pupils. One very good thing was that parents were asked to take a much more personal interest. They were now invited to come to school to meet Staff and to express their own views.

At last it was the evening for the jumps to take place. They were held in a park which had jumping pits, some way from the school and I had to rely on our team to find their way there. I was pleased to see that so many parents had come with them.

Well, what am I to say about the evening. We and our big rivals were the only schools who were represented in each contest. I did not know their Sports master very well, but I could see him looking rather surprised at our numbers. The competitors looked good too, for we had managed to supply them with new gear.

They did me and my helpers proud. As time went on, our list of winners grew until we had won almost all the High and Long jumps. The girls were doing nearly as well. By the time the evening was over, we had so many points that another school would have to win nearly all the sprints to catch us – and we still had the hurdles to go, where I knew we should pick up more points.

I noticed the rival Sports master looking at me rather quizzically and later he came over to congratulate the team. I must say he took the results in a real sportsman-like manner and when I had got to know him better, he told me, "I wondered how long it would be before someone discovered why we won each year. It's good for both of us to have some competition."

Needless to say, we did well in the hurdles, relays and sprints and ended up Boys Champions by a big margin. The girls did not quite manage to win overall, but had many successes. As my captain was presented with the trophy, I was very proud of the team, which had accomplished something that the school had never done before.

Of course, the Headmaster, who had been as nervous as I had, was delighted. When he came to congratulate the team he said, "You must come on the stage at Assembly tomorrow morning with the cup and both teams. Miss Rowland must come too with her girls."

The next morning, after normal Assembly, the teams were invited up on the platform with their trophy. You could feel the excitement and I felt that we had made another step forward.

With the Summer Term finishing in this way, we all looked forward to the holiday. I had been asked by the District Football and Athletics Committees if I would take on the post of Secretary as both of theirs had resigned. I agreed with some misgivings, but no-one else was prepared to do the job.

We all spent two weeks of our Summer holiday at Gorleston and enjoyed it as much as usual. It seemed no time at all before the Autumn Term began. This was to be a big year for us and some of our senior pupils would start their courses that could lead to the GCE O Level Examinations. We thought we were in for a quiet Term, but not likely.

One of the Senior Masters had been, as a boy, at the WSCS at Bury. I never knew him as he was about ten years older than me. When I met him at Edgware he and his wife were living in Hendon and our two families often met out of school. He travelled to school on the Edgware to Morden Underground line every day. Paul was a quiet person who everyone liked. He was content to do his teaching. He seldom took part in any other activities. I arrived home one day to find his wife on the phone. Paul had been absent and I thought she was going to tell me why. To my surprise, all she said was that he had not come home at 4 pm and did I know whether he was still at school. I must say I didn't know what to tell her and asked her to phone me if he didn't return in the next half hour.

Half an hour later she rang to say he hadn't, so I said I would drive over and see if I could help. Of course, when I got there and told her he hadn't been to school all that day she was very upset. I took her to Hendon Police Station to report him missing. One of the officers said privately to me "Had they quarrelled lately?" I said, "No, not so far as I know. Why?" He said, "We get a lot of this. A row, and the husband goes off and comes back the next day."

To cut a long story short, he didn't come back and it was about six months later that his body was found in the woods not far from Morden Station. There was no clue as to why he had got on the train that morning to Morden rather than Edgware. He had no money or home problems. It remains a mystery to this day.

Geoffrey entered Edgware Infants School at the beginning of the Spring Term. Certainly the past years had been very mixed, but he seemed a normal youngster and had heard so much about 'schools' that he was looking forward to going. The school was on the same site as the Secondary, although the entrances were quite a long distance apart. I cycled to school, or walked, so it fell to his Grandpa to take and fetch him each day. I only saw him once when I was called over because he had smashed into a window when he finished up on a slide in his classroom. Some blood and tears, but he soon recovered.

We had one more surprise that year. We were asked to stay after school for a Staff Meeting when the Head told us, rather sheepishly I thought, that he would be leaving at the end of the Summer Term. He had been appointed Education Officer for a large business firm. It was a job he couldn't afford to turn down.

I am sure all the Staff had a feeling of misgivings. Just as we were beginning to make progress – this could mean a new start. Continuous change was very bad for a school, especially when the Headmaster was liked and trusted.

This time, the new Headmaster was able to visit us during the Summer Term and to our relief Mr Cook appeared to think very much as we thought, so the school might not suffer.

Coincidences seem to be part of my life. Mr Cook turned out to be from Sudbury in Suffolk where my brother was teaching. They knew each other well. Doug assured me that he was highly thought of. What a relief!

In fact, we couldn't have asked for a better Head. The pupils liked him and our work continued as if there had been no change.

Because of my work with the District Sports Clubs I had got to know personally a large number of the Hendon Staff. One was Vic Howell, Deputy Head of Goldbeaters Secondary Modern, one station away from Edgware on the Burnt Oak Estate.

When the line had been extended to Edgware, the LCC had purchased a large piece of land around the Burnt Oak Underground Station and built an estate to house hundreds of families from the East End Boroughs of London. There, the houses were in such a position that the people who had bought quite expensive houses at Edgware and Colindale viewed the invasion with some trepidation. They needn't have worried. The newcomers settled in very quickly and soon Burnt Oak was just another station on the Edgware Line.

Of course, several new schools were built and were now a part of the Hendon Education Authority. One of these was Goldbeaters Secondary Modern Mixed, with some 350 pupils. Vic Howell had been there since its beginning. Somehow we knew very little about it as it was way off the main roads. It seemed to be just another school doing a steady unremarkable job.

Vic came from Norfolk and, as I had so many associations with the County from my holidays there, we became good friends. One day he said, "Our Head is retiring at the end of the Summer Term – why don't you apply for the post?" "I'm much too young" (I was 37). I said, "Middlesex don't appoint anyone under 40 as Head of a Secondary School." That was that, but when I began to think about it again, I wondered, "Why not. It can't do any harm. I've got new ideas about secondary education and at least the Authority will know that I have the ambition to become a Headmaster."

So, I sent in my application and to my great surprise was called for an interview! This was held at the Middlesex Education Offices in Parliament Square, so it meant a journey with plenty of time to think things over. Was I doing the right thing? I was very happy where I was, and the school in my opinion was improving all the time. Did I really want to give up actual teaching to more of an organizer? Well, I could do both and I would know who the Headmaster was, and be concerned about changes. At any rate, it was too late now and all the odds were against me.

This was a very formal interview. The candidates – there were six of us - sat together in an outer room and were called in alphabetical order. I suppose we all felt the same nervous strain for there was no conversation – we just sat there silently weighing each other up. They all appeared older than I was and would have much more experience. With my name beginning with an L, I knew I would be called somewhere in the middle of the group.

Sure enough, I was number three. I really had no idea what was before me. My predecessors remained silent when they came out.

The committee sat round a large table with an empty chair at the end for the applicant. Opposite was obviously the Chief Education Officer for

Middlesex and I had a smile from the Hendon Education Officer, whom I recognized sitting beside him. Otherwise, I did not know anyone though I expect some of the Governors of the school were there.

The Chairman introduced himself and the rest of the group, and then we got down to business. The usual first question came, "Now Mr Loades, you are applying for the Headship of Goldbeaters School – why do you think you're the right person for this post?" Considering they had seen my application and testimonials they already knew, but I suppose they wanted to hear me speak.

I told them about my views on the future of Secondary Modern education and what I would do if I were appointed. There were many questions from individuals who all told me who they were. As well as Governors, there were several advisors, one of whom was the PE Advisor, whom I knew well.

Then I was asked if I had any questions. I did ask a few, mainly about the freedom I would be given in the post. At last the Chairman said, "Thank you for applying Mr Loades. I've just got one more question for you. You say on your form that you play the piano." Seeing my puzzled look, he went on. "I can do arithmetic, but I don't call myself a mathematician – do you call yourself a musician." What a funny question, I thought, as I replied, "No Sir, just a piano player." This caused an outburst of laughter from the rest of the Committee and I thought, "I've blown it!" Then I was dismissed, and asked to stay until a decision had been made.

I rejoined the rest of the candidates who were now chatting together. "You've been a long time," one of them said. "Have I? I didn't notice,"

I replied – and then silence descended again while the interviews continued. At last, they were finished and we sat waiting for the result.

It was not very long before the Clerk came in and after thanking us all for coming said, "Mr. Loades, the Committee would like to see you again." I knew I had been successful. What a surprise!

The Chairman and Committee congratulated me and wished me success. My Education Officer said he would be seeing me soon and I expressed my pleasure. The last words to me were, "You will be the youngest Secondary Headmaster in Middlesex," and I rushed off to find a telephone and tell Betty the good news.

When I returned to Edgware School the next day, I didn't know exactly how I felt. I had been very happy there and the members of Staff were almost personal friends, but they all seemed pleased for me and I knew that a new chapter in my life was about to begin.

Chapter 11
GOLDBEATERS SCHOOL 1951

I had one big advantage in going to Goldbeaters. My Deputy Head, Vic Howell, was a personal friend. The rest of the Staff, except for the PE Master who I had met on various sports occasions, I knew nothing about. I met Vic there one evening after school, just to see what it was like.

The building was two-storied and tucked around a corner away from the main road. It was reasonably modern and had Woodwork, Domestic Science, Science and Needlework rooms. There were seventeen Staff, nine men and eight ladies. Most of them were very experienced and had been there for several years. I wanted to meet them and asked if they would be prepared to stay after school one day. Vic said he was sure they would – he would arrange it.

Before I met them, I had what I considered was a strange telephone message from another Hendon Headmaster. I had never met him and after he had introduced himself he congratulated me and then said, "You are very young – thirty seven. Now you can sit back for twenty three years and do nothing!" I thought, "Thank goodness I'm not on your Staff if that's your idea of education."

We had a pleasant meeting – their old Head had been there for a long time and had assembled a well-ordered and hardworking Staff, who had slipped behind in modern thinking. I felt the pupils were really standing still and I intended to open up opportunities for them – tactfully of course.

I don't like to be talking about 'me' all the time, but it is my story and the new ideas were mine, so I will quote what one of the Senior Masters said when I moved six years later to another Headship. Mr. Marlow, Head of the Science Department, said to the local newspaper, "We thought that the school was already perfect when Mr. Loades came to us but he introduced a new element by giving the children more responsibility and he brought into being a most successful 'Prefect System'. He also introduced the 'House System' to give an incentive for pupils to give their best not only for themselves. He has been most active himself, especially on the sports side. In the old days, we rather drifted but we now have great aims. The GCE 'O' Level is now a regular thing. Our first success was three years ago and now children in a Secondary Modern School are doing things of which they were not thought capable, because they were never given the chance."

We made sure that the less-able pupil would not suffer because of an emphasis on the brighter ones. We built up a partnership with the local Technical College and, what I thought was most important, a great relationship with the parents. They were not used to coming to school to discuss matters with the Staff but once they found we were approachable a new feeling of partnership spread through the school. We made sure that employment advisors visited us each Term of their last year and parents and pupils were given the chance to talk to them and me about their futures – what they wanted to do and how to prepare for it.

I know this became quite usual several years later, but I like to think we were one of the first schools to use the system.

Actually my first Term at Goldbeaters did not start well at all. I had to have an operation. Four weeks' stay in the hospital was a big gap in the

Term, but I arrived back to find the school running very smoothly under its Deputy Head.

One of the things I wanted to do was arrange a school journey. Our children did not get much chance to travel and this was something they should experience. I'd had a new member of Staff sent to me during the Autumn Term. He was in his late forties and could help out in many ways. I hadn't asked for him and assumed the office would take him away when they had a vacancy. As we got to know him better we learned that he had won the VC in the 2nd World War. He never talked about it, but somehow we all knew.

When he heard of my interest in school journeys he came to me and offered to organize one for late in the Spring Term. He said he knew a school in Belgium that we could use as a base and he would arrange trips from there. I talked it over with the Staff and decided to go ahead. We had no difficulty in getting pupils wanting to go from the 3rd year and he arranged for the money to be paid in each week to cover expenses. The trip was to take place in the last-but-one week before the Easter holidays. They would leave here on a Sunday morning, cross the Channel by ferry and be picked up by a coach in Belgium.

Early Saturday morning before they were to leave, I had a phone call from Mr. Smith – not his real name – to say could he come and see me and talk about final arrangements. He didn't live far away so I said "Yes, but I would be seeing them off from the railway station in the morning." He said there was no need to do that, if he called today. He came and we had quite a long talk arranging for a phone call when they arrived in Belgium. I was impressed with the way he had organized things.

About an hour later I had a phone call. There was a lady on the line who said Mr. Smith hadn't returned home yet – was he still with me? I asked, "Are you Mrs. Smith?" "No, she said, but we live together. I'm a nurse at Edgware Hospital."

I told her he had come to see me about his trip to Belgium tomorrow. She said she knew nothing about such a journey. Alarm bells were beginning to ring in my head, and I asked her to call me again if he wasn't back in an hour. She did so to say that she was very worried – and so was I.

Being a Saturday there was no-one at the Education Office and no-one at school to turn to. The only thing I could think of was to ring the Belgian Embassy and tell them the facts and ask them to contact their school. The answer came very soon – there was no school of that name in Belgium.

The only thing I could do then was to visit the pupils' homes and tell their parents the trip was off. It was late afternoon and they were very scattered over North London – it was going to take a long time.

Betty came with me and we finished the last call at midnight. We could not stay long anywhere and it was one of the worst experiences of my life. Many of them had had a bath and were in bed and there were tears and some recriminations. We were exhausted when we got home.

I was at the Education Office at Hendon when it opened on Monday morning. How could I have been so naïve and gullible to let his happen?

The Chief Education Officer was naturally surprised to see me, but sympathetic when I told him my story. He said he would call a meeting of the Governors that evening and send letters to all the parents saying what he was doing. There was also a meeting of the Education Committee and he would see them too.

It was no good being miserable and doing nothing so it was back to school and a Staff Meeting. I would tell the pupils that the journey had had to be cancelled without going into details. I also sent letters out to all the parents concerned, without too many details, saying I would see them as soon as I had any news.

Next morning, the Chief phoned me up and said the Governors and Committee were sympathetic, did not blame me, and would refund any money the parents had lost. They were also informing the police and the 'Missing Persons Bureau'.

This was wonderful news, which I was able to give to the parents at my meeting with them. They really didn't blame me – I blamed myself. I had decided that we would have a school journey next year and I would take it myself with the help of the RI Master and Betty. I would keep a close watch over the plans. Now all we could do was wait for 'Mr. Smith' to turn up and hear his side of the story.

That Summer, we went to the Isle of Wight for our holiday. I was sitting on the beach at Ventnor one morning reading the paper when I saw the headline "Teacher Reports to the Police". Sure enough it was 'Mr. Smith' who had walked into an Oxford Police Station and told his story.

Later he was charged with taking the money and given a heavy fine. Someone in the Court heard he had the VC and paid his fine for him, and he left a free man. That was it, I thought, but not quite. A few weeks later, the Education Officer came to see me and after general conversation said, " 'Mr. Smith' is back here and wants to teach again. Will you take him back on your Staff?" I cannot think why anyone should consider it possible that he could return to work with those he had let down so badly, so my answer was a definite "No". I think he expected this because he didn't try to persuade me otherwise. I never heard what happened to 'Mr. Smith', thank goodness.

As I have said, it wasn't a very good start to my Headship, but things quietened down and we began to develop ideas. I couldn't have asked for a more cooperative Staff and parents, and we all looked forward to the future.

The school journey to Ireland was much enjoyed. We went by coach to Liverpool and crossed to Belfast by ferry, staying at a school camp when we arrived. My RI Master had arranged visits for every day, including one to Dublin where we were welcomed by the Mayor. When we returned, we gave an exhibition to the parents and pupils of what we had done. I felt a great weight lifted from my shoulders.

We took mother and father down to stay with Ada for the Easter holiday and left them there for a while. We were shocked when father collapsed and died suddenly, and to make matters worse a few months later Billie died too.

To her dismay, Ada found that the house, which she had paid for, was in Billie's name. He had a family, of which she knew nothing, who turned up claiming the house and its contents. This was a very distressing time for us all. There she was with nothing but her teacher's pension. There was only one thing to do – bring her back to live with us at Edgware. In those days, families looked after their own and it was unthinkable to put her in a home. At any rate, she and her sister had always got on well together and they would be company for each other.

As it turned out, mother lived until she was eighty-seven and Ada until ninety-seven – she died a year before I retired. At least we never had to worry about a baby sitter, but at the same time we never had a house to ourselves until I retired. We were fortunate though that they were both easy people to live with, and we were very fond of them.

At this time, a new Secondary Modern School was being built in Hendon at Mill Hill. It was on a beautiful site and had all the facilities you required. I would have liked nothing better than to be its Head but I had only been at Goldbeaters for three years so it would have been unfair to leave just as our plans were beginning to mature. The choice was taken out of my hands when I was asked by a member of the Education Committee to apply. I talked it over with my Deputy Head, and he thought the same – he said the chance might never come again.

My application was made with some trepidation – even more so when I was called for the interview. However, I needn't have worried – I didn't get the job. It's strange to feel relieved when you've failed, but I did. I was told later that the Committee was unhappy about me leaving Goldbeaters so soon, and they appointed a member of the Staff of a Training College whose experience of a living with a school was minimal. The final twist was that my Deputy Head was given the Deputy Headship at the new school when it opened.

So things went smoothly on their way with satisfying results until – I'm always talking about the way fate takes over our lives and here it was again.

I had a phone call from a Haringey Headmaster who said he had heard about the work we were doing and was very interested. Could he come and see me? Of course, I said "Yes". He probably would have ideas of his own, which would be useful. I checked the area the Haringey Authority covered and found that it was very wide and scattered. It was just outside the LCC and covered Highgate, with its famous Public School, Tottenham, Hornsey, Wood Green and Muswell Hill, with a mixed population. His school was in Muswell Hill on the edge of Finchley.

He came, a man in his early fifties. We talked and I showed him around. He did not tell me much about his own school but as he left he asked if I would like to visit, and I arranged to go the following week.

The journey from home by car took only thirty minutes. The shock came when I got out of the car. The entrance to William Grimshaw School was magnificent. It was obviously a new building, only two or three years old. The palatial entrance hall housed an interesting art display and I could see a very large Assembly hall attached.

I said to the Head when I met him, "You didn't tell me you had such a new school!" "Yes, it's only three years old. It cost a quarter of a million to build." This was an enormous sum in those days. "I'll show you around before we talk", he said.

On the ground floor there was this grand entrance leading into a very large Assembly Hall, with stage, lighting gallery and Green Room. The kitchens were here for school dinners. To the other side was a beautiful Library, Secretary's room , Head's and Deputy's rooms, and the Staff Room

A wide corridor from the entrance on the ground floor led to a Gymnasium, with showers, and the Science Laboratories.

Upstairs was a large Art Department, and Domestic Science, Needlework, Music and Commercial rooms, well fitted-out with office equipment. Here, there were also the General Subjects rooms, for English, Mathematics, History, Geography, Religious Instruction, etc. – all well equipped. In fact, it was a Headmaster's dream.

The more I saw, the more I was impressed by the opportunities that were offered. Behind the building was a large playing field, a hard Athletics track, and grass Soccer, Rugby, Hockey and Cricket pitches. Across the playground, there was also a Practical Centre – Woodwork, Metalwork and Pottery.

In all, the school would hold about six hundred pupils.

We went back to the Head's office with me in somewhat of a daze. I told him that he had a school with facilities I'd always wanted. He looked me rather strangely and said, "I'll let you in on a secret. I'm leaving at the end of the Term to become an Inspector in the Midlands – why don't you apply for it? The advertisement will be out next week."

"I wouldn't stand a chance," I said. "I'm much too young and inexperienced."

"Well", he said, "you seem to have done well so far or I wouldn't have heard about you. Think about it."

We went on to discuss the work at Goldbeaters and when I left, he said again, "Give it serious thought." I did!

I had been at Goldbeaters six years and achieved about all I could with the facilities I had. As long as I kept the Staff then everything could run smoothly. I could sit back, as had been suggested by my phone caller, and do nothing for the next seventeen years. I decided not to tell Betty or anyone else about William Grimshaw until it was advertised. Even then I should think there would be tremendous competition for the job from all over the country.

The advertisement duly appeared the next week and without telling anyone I sent for an application form. If I failed, no one need know of my dreams.

I had almost forgotten the whole thing when, in the middle of the Summer Term I was asked to go for an interview. Still, I told no-one and went to the Haringey Education Office as if I was going to school as usual. I had told my Deputy that I might be a bit late in but that was all.

I won't bore you with an account of the interview. This time I was out of my home territory – I knew no-one when I walked into the room. It seemed the usual type of interview, although I found someone had been doing his homework when questions were asked.

Finally, the Haringey Education Officer said, "Your own school seems to be progressing very well – why do you want to leave?" I said, "I don't want to leave really, but the facilities at William Grimshaw are so good that I should be able to fulfil my ambitions if I am Headmaster there."

To cut a long story short, I was offered the post – which I accepted immediately, and went home, rather bemused, to tell the Staff and Betty. The latter was very pleased of course. Without her interest and support I couldn't do the work I wanted and she was always encouraging me. I found it much more difficult to tell the Staff at school. I really was happy there and knew them and their families so well. One of them said, "I knew we shouldn't keep you long." Whether that was a criticism or a compliment I'm not sure! They all wished me well and I said that if they wanted to move I had a vacancy.

During the last few pages if I have not written of our home life very much. I can assure you that it was a happy and active one. Geoffrey had moved onto Orange Hill Grammar School, which was not far away. Often he and I would cycle together on the same route in the morning. He was showing promise at cricket and hoping to play in the District team. We were still going to Edgware Church, and he joined the Scout Troup and grew very attached to it.

The Scouts were a well-run outfit that had an excellent Brass Band. Geoffrey learned to play the trumpet and every month we would follow him marching through Edgware from their headquarters for a Church Parade. The band was so good that it appeared in a Ralph Reader Gang Show on television. We all enjoyed the activities that took place. The Annual Fete, to raise money for the camping, was held on the Edgware Town Football Club ground and as many as two thousand people would turn up. Betty and I played our part in running a stall – I remember it now – it was a balloon race, and the exciting part was when the gas- filled balloons were returned – often from Europe.

Our Summer holidays were more varied now since Ada had left Gorleston. We did go back with my brother and his family a few times and stayed in digs. I could afford a better car now and we ventured to take the journey, and it was a long one, to my sister and her family at Ulverston in Cumbria. Her husband, Harry, was Headmaster of a local Primary School and she was on his Staff. Their three children, Alan, Peter and Linda all intended to be teachers. Harry was born in the Lake District and knew it like the back of his hand. With seven of us in one car we had some wonderful trips and came to love the lakes, as most people seem to do when they get to know the area.

Harry was a great sportsman and played cricket for one of the League Clubs in the area and Rugby League for Barrow. One year, they reached the Rugby League Cup Final at Wembley, and of course we all went. I'd never seen a Rugby League match before and looked forward to it. In the event, it was a disappointment. Barrow never seemed to hold the ball for long and were well beaten. I've never been to another Rugby League match since – only seen it on television.

When I returned from holiday that year, I would be embarking on an entirely new experience.

(20) Cousins in Putney, London, SW13, who gave us shelter after WWII, 1945

(21) Our home in Hazel Gardens, Edgware, Middlesex, 1945

(22) The Staff of Edgware Secondary School, 1946

(23) The house of Auntie Ada and Uncle Billy on the cliff-top at Gorleston-on-Sea

(24) Cricket at low tide on the beach at Gorleston

(25) My family circa. 1948

(26) Geoffrey, Charles and Betty on the Promenade at Gorleston, circa. 1950

(27) Charles Loades' first Headship Goldbeaters Secondary Modern, 1951

(28) Charles Loades' second Headship William Grimshaw Secondary Modern, 1957

Chapter 12

WILLIAM GRIMSHAW SECONDARY MODERN SCHOOL
1957

Obviously I could not neglect Goldbeaters in my last Term there but I had to meet the Grimshaw Staff and let them meet me. The only way I could do it was to leave a bit early one afternoon and ask them to stay behind for a meeting. The Deputy Head, Mr Shirley, had been interviewed with me and we got on well together then. I don't think he really expected to become Head, and we had travelled back home together discussing the future. I contacted him asking what he thought. He was sure the Staff would want to meet me and he would arrange it.

So it was that I held my first Staff Meeting at William Grimshaw. I had learned that Sir William Grimshaw had been a great educationalist in Haringey and the school was named in his honour.

I only had fourteen Staff at Goldbeaters so when I met the new group it was like addressing a whole school – there were over forty of them.

I did not want to express my views at this stage so I had asked for it to be kept informal. We had a cup of tea together and then I met the Heads of Departments with their Staff. There was no time to go into details now, so I asked them what they thought about future meetings. After some discussion, we agreed that I would come over after school several times and meet each Department separately. I could probably manage two at each visit. It would mean a lot of travelling for me, but I didn't mind that. I just had to know how the school was working before we made a new timetable for the Autumn Term. The Head gave me a copy of the present timetable.

This worked much better than I expected. The only afternoon I did not go was Friday and in three weeks I had seen everybody.

The general feeling I got was that they thought the school was underperforming. Perhaps the present Head had known he was going and had not been prepared to look to the future. I did know he was always very pleasant and let me hold any out-of-school meetings that I wanted. The Practical Departments felt particularly that with their excellent facilities they should be doing better. Sometimes I thought that they had heard what Goldbeaters, working under great difficulties on the Practical side, had managed to do. All Departments wanted to use what they had to the best advantage to the pupils. At least I started with one big PLUS – the enthusiasm was there. All I had to do was use it.

I also met quite a number of the senior pupils. There was not yet a 6th Form, and never would be under the present conditions, but I found them courteous and concerned about their own futures.

There were only two vacancies for Staff for the Autumn – a Deputy Headmistress and Head of Pottery. I had no difficulty in filling the vacancies. I was particularly pleased with the young man who applied for the Pottery post. His experience and examples of his pupil's work were just what I wanted. As his wife was joining the Grammar School Staff, we expected him to stay for some time, in fact he was with me seventeen years later when I retired. I have some of his pupils' work at home still, which brings back fond memories.

With the help of the Heads of Departments I worked out a Timetable for the Autumn Term, although we all knew there would be changes – possibly before the end of the year.

As usual we went to Norfolk for our Summer holiday. Mother did not want to travel these days so we left her and Ada with an old friend, who regarded looking after them as a holiday. I enjoyed the holiday, but at the back of my mind was the thought that I would be going back to meet five hundred children I didn't know and Staff that I barely knew! Oh well, it was my own choice so no-one else could be blamed.

After my holiday, I went to school several times to make sure I knew my way around. We were going to have an Assembly starting later than usual to give everyone a chance to settle down. With the school being based on a Departmental subject basis for registration, all the Staff would have a new form group, but would keep their old rooms.

Remember, we had 120 new first-year pupils who were just as nervous, and probably more so, then I was.

We could not seat everybody and the older pupils had to stand, with their Form Teachers, towards the back of the hall. The rest of the Staff sat on the stage with me. When all were ready, my Deputy called me and there was silence as I went onto the stage.

I wanted everything to be as informal as possible and yet under control. I had seen so many Assemblies, when I was an Assistant, where there was shuffling and whispering and I felt they were not worth having. Junior schools all seemed to have the same procedures. The Head would say 'Good morning children,' and in a sing-song unison the school answered

'Good morning Mr Jones, good morning teachers'. All I needed was a 'Good morning school' from me and a 'Good morning Sir' reply, said in natural voices.

I then told them how pleased I was to be their new Headmaster and I was looking forward to the future. As I looked at them as a school I realised that we had quite a mixture of nationalities, and I hoped we could devise an Assembly which would suit them all, without offending anyone. I knew that some schools had separate Assemblies with, for instance, the Jewish pupils meeting by themselves, with a Jewish teacher. I wanted to avoid this if possible.

I then introduced the new Members of Staff and talked about the Term to come, then all but the First Years left to return to their form rooms for Timetables and other matters. After lunch, we would begin the new Timetable.

They left in an orderly fashion and I was quite pleased with the first Assembly. The new pupils with their Form Teachers remained behind. Miss Oliver, the new Deputy, stayed too, and we tried to make them feel at home as we answered questions and explained how the school worked. Of course, we were all new, but they had had the opportunity to come and see the school with their parents at the end of the previous Term.

So ended my first Assembly, except that one of the senior boys come up to me as I left and said, "Excuse me, Sir, but do you come from Australia?" "No," I said, "What made you think that?" "Well you have a slight sing-song in your voice, just as the Australians have." I knew what that meant. "Oh, I said. That's the Suffolk dialect!"

At Goldbeaters, my room had been upstairs tucked away in a corner and I saw nobody all day unless they came specially to see me. Here, I was by the main entrance so I saw all visitors coming and going. The passage outside led to the Library and the Staff Room and was in continuous use. Not that it was noisy, just continuous movement. I found this most disconcerting. With the two Secretaries, only a door away, I never seemed to have a moment of quietness to myself. It took me a whole Term to get used to it.

Haringey Borough Council hovered between Conservative and Labour. My Governors were a mixture of the two political Parties and that was a great advantage. It meant that whichever party was in power had the most members as Governors, but any change in numbers was minimal. I got used to having a slight change in the balance of power after an election, but it really meant the same people over and over again, with a new Chairman.

They were excellent. They were very proud of Grimshaw and helped in every possible way. I was allowed to choose my own candidates for a vacancy and at the interviews it was the Head of Department and I that decided who would get the Post. Only once, several years later, did they go against my wishes – but more of that later. The same set of Governors acted for Tollington Grammar School, which was on the same site, only a playing-field away. The Chairman of the Education Committee was a middle-aged lady who had lived in this part of the East End of London all her life, and had the accent and the warm heartedness that goes with the area. She often visited me by herself, and was a great help in getting my proposals accepted by the Committee.

Things went quite well, and almost before we realized it, Christmas was upon us. The Art Department invited me to go with them to the Children's Ward at the local hospital to put up decorations that they had made. Evidently this was something they did every year and I was pleased to accept. They had big cut-out painted Christmas figures to put in the windows and masses of holly and mistletoe. With a Christmas tree and coloured lights, the ward was transformed and it was great to see the pleasure in the faces of the young patients.

As I write this, I am watching the News on TV and hear that hospital wards will not be decorated this year because of the risk of infection. Our visit was fifty years ago, when evidently there were no such problems.

I had had the idea for some time that a school should try and help the older, poorer citizens in its area and this was the time of year to do it. If every class could provide a parcel of groceries, these would be much appreciated. I contacted Social Services. They thought it was an excellent idea, and would send me a list of names and addresses. The Staff and pupils thought so too, and set about collecting empty boxes from all the shops in Muswell Hill. In the end, we had enough groceries to fill over two hundred boxes – wrapped in Christmas paper, they looked very festive and it was agreed to close early on the last afternoon of Term for them to be delivered by small groups of pupils.

That this was appreciated was in no doubt, going by the many letters of thanks I received. It also had a spin-off that we had not expected. Having seen that the old people had problems getting out to do their shopping, many pupils offered to go back after Christmas and help, and this they then did for several years. I was pleased that a Parents' Evening with Carols and Readings ended the Term and I went home with a feeling that, on the whole, my first Term had gone well.

I don't intend to go through the school year week-by-week. After the Christmas holiday, we returned knowing that we were working towards our goal of giving all our pupils the chance of a choice of subjects when they reached the Third Year, but until then their programme would include a range of practical subjects such as Art, Woodwork, Metalwork, Needlework and Domestic Science all being available for both boys and girls. After that, with the GCE in view, they could specialize more in two years' time. Technical Drawing and Commercial Studies would be introduced and contacts made with Hornsey School of Art and the Technical College.

I was very fortunate in having first-class Heads of Departments in all these subjects. I had a new young master for Music and hoped to bring in Drama later.

I had heard from my brother that Dad was not very well and to my dismay he had a heart attack and died. We went to Bury for the funeral, which was held in St. Mary's Church where he had been a choir boy. Once again, a sad time. He had been a very good father. My stepmother was returning to her family in Cheshire.

The Music teacher was proving his worth and wanted to put on a concert for the parents. This was a great success and in the discussion afterwards the idea was put forward that if we had a Drama teacher we could put on a musical play. At that time Gilbert and Sullivan Operettas had made a return to popularity and some of these were ideal for schools.

I knew just the person I wanted. I'm not going to give her real name. I'll just call her 'Jane'. She had been on the Staff at Edgware School with me for a time and then moved to Primary work. We had been to see some of her productions and they were excellent. I wondered if she would like to return to Secondary work and teach English and Drama. I phoned her up and invited her to come and see me. She came and was impressed, and when I had a vacancy she joined us. Now we were all set for next year's production.

During the Summer Term, I was invited by some members of Staff to join them on a Saturday morning for a game of golf. I did play, but not very well because I'd never had the time – but they said neither did they, they just played for the fun of it. None of us were members of a Club so could go to one of many clubs near us and pay the green fees.

One of the players was our Religious Instruction Master. He was in his fifties and a qualified minister who was having a change from Parish work. We were chatting as we walked round when he said, "I understand you often go to Norfolk. I'm going to Mundesley tomorrow – do you know it?" I told him I had driven through the village but never stopped – my visits were more south to Gorleston and Yarmouth. He said, "I've a caravan at Mundesley which I'm selling and a possible buyer is meeting me there tomorrow." I still don't know to this day why I said, "Well, if he doesn't buy it, can I see it?" "Of course", was the reply.

Back at school on Monday he came to me and said he hadn't sold the caravan. "How about you and your wife going down next weekend, taking some sleeping bags, and staying a couple of nights?"

I hadn't mentioned this to Betty and she was just as surprised as I was. Still, she was quite happy to have a weekend by the sea. We would take Geoffrey. Auntie and Mother were quite capable of looking after themselves.

We travelled down on the Friday evening and found the journey a pleasant one. As we lived on the outskirts of London we were in the country as soon as we started. It was still light when we arrived.

The site was called Kiln Cliffs and lay on the top of the cliffs on the edge of the village. Years ago, it had been a brick-making works and the Brick Kiln, now an office, stood in the centre. A brick storage shed was the caravan shop during the Spring and Summer. At that time all the caravans had to be removed at the end of October and returned by Easter. It was in a beautiful position, hidden from the main road with access down the cliffs by way of steps to a wide sandy beach.

There was no electricity except in the toilets, showers and washroom. The caravans were lit by Calor Gas, which was also used for cooking. A small open fire was the heating and water had to be drawn from a stand-pipe and stored in a plastic canister. No refrigerator - but we never bought food in bulk. This all sounds very basic but in fact it was very comfortable and you soon became used to it.

You will have gathered by now that we bought the caravan. It could comfortably house six people. The owner of the site's daughter still runs the park fifty years later – it has been modernized with electricity and running water and is one of the best in the district.

The purchase changed our lives as far as holidays were concerned. From then on, we spent every holiday there, except Christmas, and often went for weekends with friends. The park was mainly used by families and we all got to know each other very well. Our children grew up together, and although it was fifty years ago we still send Christmas cards to each other.

We soon got to know the village and the people of Mundesley very well – little did we guess that we would come to live here when I retired.

We also managed other holidays. Thank goodness for 12 weeks' holiday a year. Usually, Geoffrey's friend Peter came with us. While writing this I happen to be watching the Remembrance service for the Manchester United football players who lost their lives in the plane accident at Munich airport. It was 50 years ago, and a week after it happened we went for a holiday to Yugoslavia, taking Peter with us.

We flew from the small airport of Southend in a Dakota, which may today seem a strange thing to do, but we had booked the tour through Travel Agents and this was their decision. The Dakota, propeller driven, had been used in World War II to transport troops and was not a large plane, but a safe one. From where I sat, I could see the exhausts from the two engines and as we began to leave the coastline behind us, they were already white hot. I presumed this was normal and didn't like to ask the pilot – but it was a little worrying.

Then we were told that we would break our flight at Munich to re-fuel. The runway seemed to stretch out forever and the stewards showed us where the Manchester United plane had crashed on take-off just a week or so earlier. You can imagine how we felt when we left. Nonetheless, we proceeded to have a good holiday in Yugoslavia, despite the fact that the country was still recovering from the War.

We spent several Easter holidays in Paris staying with French friends whose daughter had previously come to live with us in Edgware for six months to learn English. We had remained close friends and Paris in the Springtime is a marvellous place.

For holidays during those years we branched out to a variety of different places - touring Scotland towing a caravan, staying in a Welsh village, and even taking the train to Austria, then on to Lido di Jessolo and Venice in Northern Italy. All were very much enjoyed.

At school, there was so much to do that time slipped by unnoticed. Jane joined us, and fitted in very well. *Trial by Jury* was staged in the Spring Term to great acclaim. Some of the male Staff joined the chorus, which encouraged senior boys, and with an orchestra strengthened by outside help it was quite a professional production. These musicals continued for several years, interspersed with plays.

The most memorable production was *A Midsummer Night's Dream* staged in an open space behind the school with a backing of shrubs and trees. We could seat about three hundred parents, but each night the grass had to be sprayed with repellent to keep down the insects. The weather was perfect and, just to finish it off, a full moon hung over Muswell Hill as if it was part of the scenery. The Technical Department lit the path from school with coloured bulbs that added even more atmosphere to the scene. The weather was ideal and I shall never forget the scene when the fairies, all First-Year children, emerged from the bushes in the darkness each holding a coloured light.

I was so thrilled with the evening that I thought it was worth doing again to a different audience. My close friend from College, Eric MacAllister, was Head of a village school in the depths of Hertfordshire. I told him about the show and asked if he would like us to come on a Saturday evening and perform for his school in their gardens. We would welcome anybody who wanted to come from the village. There would be no charge. I knew he would love the idea for he had the same ideas about education as I did. Of course he said "yes", and now I had to see if the Staff agreed. Everybody was pleased to perform again. We hired a coach and left home late-morning. Several of the parents were coming by car. The journey took about an hour and we would have time to prepare after a quiet lunch.

We were fortunate in that it was a fine day and the afternoon passed quickly as the acting area was chosen. Some chairs were available for the older spectators – the rest would have to sit on the grass or stand.

As the starting time approached, more and more people arrived from the local village until there was a large audience, and as it began to get dark the play began.

Once again it was a huge success. The cast excelled themselves and we had a great evening. We left for home about ten o'clock amidst a storm of cheers and by the time we reached Haringey most of the pupils had to be awakened to go to bed – I was nearly in the same state.

By now, the school was running smoothly and looking forward to our first entries into the GCE examinations in a year's time. The CSE had also come into use, where the actual class-work was taken into account as well as the exams, which was an added incentive.

At about this time, as was happening all over the country, we had our first experience with drugs. A mother had written saying her daughter had seen a girl passing something to another girl before she ran in a race, and she was worried it might be drugs. I had the two girls together with the Senior Mistress but soon found that all they had been doing was passing sweets to each other.

However, I had been hearing and reading of cases where drug dealers had approached pupils on their way out of school during the day. Although half of our pupils stayed for lunch there were still a large number who brought sandwiches or went home. Unloading large numbers of children on Muswell Hill for an hour at mid-day could cause problems, although we had very few complaints from shopkeepers. However, as you have probably gathered, I like to deal with problems before they develop and, although I knew the newspapers would probably have headlines like "Local School has Drug Problems," I invited parents to come to a meeting to talk about the subject. When the evening came, there was a full meeting – parents had read so much about the drug problem that they were pleased to hear the truth.

I believe it is best to discuss these things rather than try to hide them. As it was, we had nothing to hide although it is impossible, with six hundred children, to cover every possibility. I did ask that no parent should try to hide a problem, but that we would tackle it together.

In some ways we could encourage staying in school at lunchtime rather than wandering around the shops. An ice-cream van was always parked in a road outside the entrance and attracted customers who afterwards strayed away. The owner of the van was delighted when I allowed him to bring his van into the school playground during the lunch period. In fact, he was so pleased that he made a donation to the school every month and there was no more criticism from local householders.

We also held lunchtime concerts and film shows and I have to thank the 6th Form for these. One favourite was a guitar soloist who performed regularly. As I sat and listened to him - his name was Ray Davies - I never guessed that when he left school he would form the group called "The Kinks", with two others from the school and a friend from the Art College. They were one of the most popular bands of the 1970s, and they kept in touch with me. Another pupil at the school around the same time, also destined to become a world famous singing artist, was Rod Stewart.

I am pleased to say that, with the co-operation of parents, we had no serious drug problems. I realize that drug abuse was only in its infancy then, and not the menace it became later.

Mother and Auntie Ada were still living with us, although Ada was confined to her bedroom because of the stairs difficulty. Sadly, mother passed away, peacefully, when she was 87. She had been like my own mother to me, and I had much to thank her for.

Just a word or two here about my son, Geoffrey, at around this time, and what he went on to do. He left Grammar School in 1961 and went straight into a three-year management trainee course with the Beecham Group, famous for brands like Brylcreem and Macleans toothpaste. At the same time, he gained a degree in Business Studies, which all gave him a very good start in the business world. From there, his career in marketing with companies such as Colgate-Palmolive led him to be appointed Director of the International Gold Corporation in London, later to become the World Gold Council. In 1989, he moved with his family to the world headquarters in Geneva, Switzerland, where they are still living, and he works now as a consultant to various international organizations and governments. Sussi, my daughter-in-law, is at the Danish Mission to the United Nations in Geneva, and their daughter, Emma, my grand-daughter, is an Associate Director at the World Economic Forum, famous among other things for its Annual Meeting of world leaders in Davos, Switzerland. It seems hardly possible that Geoffrey is now sixty-six years old, and that they are all doing such important, interesting things – none of them teaching!

Life at William Grimshaw continued very smoothly, with our 6th Form growing each year and children from all over Haringey joining us. I tried to make sure that all our pupils felt they were being cared for – not just the intelligent ones. With this in mind, we did not reward just those who came top in examinations, but those that did other things for the school as well.

I had sat through so many boring prize-givings, both as a pupil myself and as a member of Staff, that I wanted something more interesting. With this in mind, the fist requirement was a good speaker, and someone who would not just talk about the value of a good education – we could do that ourselves – but more. Michael Aspel and Richard Baker were the BBC newsreaders at nearby Alexandra Palace and both of them came – but not together. Another year it was the lady who was the winner of *Brain of Britain* on BBC radio. I was often criticised, but not by the Staff, for not encouraging more competition between individuals. The mentally bright would always come out top in examinations, but there is more than this if you really want a happy and responsible life. I was certainly never in the 'very bright' class myself, but I still enjoyed a full life mainly concerned with helping others.

It was now the 2nd half of the 1960s. Education was in the news and the word 'Comprehensive' seemed to be on everyone's lips. The Labour government wanted to drop the 'Eleven Plus' examination and do away with Grammar Schools. The LCC had already started. All I knew was that the new schools were always large – usually over a thousand pupils - and intended to give everyone as full an education as possible.

It all sounded very much like William Grimshaw, though with the Grammar Schools disappearing you could expect a larger proportion of academic pupils. A cousin of mine who was working at one such school within the LCC was enthusiastic about the results. Her Headmistress - it was an all-girls' school - was later made a Dame as a result of her efforts.

In 1967, we were told we would be 'going Comprehensive' in the Autumn. Grimshaw and Tollington, which were sited very close together (as you see from the aerial photograph), were to become one school. This would mean a school of 1400 pupils – the largest in the Borough. It also meant that the new school would be under one Headmaster. The general policy was that any present Head Teachers who lost their posts due to the merging of schools would be paid their old salaries, and, if they wished to stay, would become Deputy Heads. As you can imagine, there were a lot of worried Heads at that time. Appointments of Staff would be made by Easter 1967, and present Heads would be released from their duties for the Summer Term to appoint their new Staff and organize the new school. Ours would have a new name too – Creighton School, the name of the road in which it stood.

Four years prior to this, a brand new Tollington had been built next to the old building. Of course, it had all the facilities that we had, except for the Practical subjects. I wondered if someone knew what was going to happen and had made sure that both buildings could offer the best facilities at the same time.

The Grammar School Head and I knew each other well, and we applied for the same post. Somehow I did not worry as much as I expected to about the interview. Both of us knew the Governors – I had known them for ten years. By now they must have made up their minds as to which of us they wanted.

The interview was held at the Education Office with the Director of Education there as well. It was quite straight forward – like meeting old friends – and I was called back to be offered the job. As I commiserated with the other Head, he said, "Don't worry – I don't really want a Comprehensive. I've got an interview for a Grammar School Headship next week and I think I shall get it." He did.

Immediately after the Easter break my task of choosing Staff began. My Deputy, Miss Oliver, wanted to move to a Girls' School and there was a vacancy which she accepted. Now I had to choose both a male and a female Deputy. The latter was easy. The present Deputy at Tollington had only a few years before she retired. It would be cruel to return her to the ordinary Staff. I knew she was a capable woman, and even if she didn't agree with Comprehensive Education she would do her best.

The choice of a Deputy Headmaster was more difficult. I looked through the list of those who would be left without a school. There was only one who I had met before. He was from the other side of the Borough, and one year had invited me on a trip he did every year with his Geography Department. I was impressed. He hired a helicopter – a large one – and the group were taken for a trip over their own district with a running commentary being given by the Geography Master.

I found it very interesting and so did the class. I must say I worried that the propeller might suddenly stop and we would drop like a stone down to the ground – or would parachutes attached to the plane suddenly be released and we would float safely down and land on the Tottenham Hotspurs football pitch?

Of course we landed safely, but I've never been in a helicopter since.

I talked to Ron Fielding and asked him what he intended to do. He said one or two Heads had approached him, but none he would like to work under. I invited him to spend a day with me. This he did, having an opportunity to speak to Staff and pupils and walk round the school himself.

When he came back I told him what I wanted him to do. He would be in charge of the South Wing – the old Grammar School – and teach mathematics. He had just completed a course on the latter and I knew he was right up-to-date with modern maths teaching. He had told me that he liked making up Timetables. This was a difficult job and every Head had his own way of doing it. Computers were not available in those days. Today, I presume every Head has one that makes the task much easier. I suggested he give himself time to think it over – I had already decided I wanted him to come.

I felt that I needed to visit some Comprehensives that had been in action for a time to see how they were doing. It was interesting but no two schools were the same – it depended so much on the area in which they were situated. I had a message for me from Ron asking to come and see me again, and he came and said he would like the job. I told him how pleased I was and how important his presence would be. With the Deputy Headmistress leaving in a short time he would have to take on the whole responsibility if I was not available.

I wanted now to put to my Deputies my ideas on how the new school would be organized. The 6th Form, which would grow all the time, I hoped, would be the responsibility of a 6th Form Tutor. The rest would be divided vertically into six groups – call them Houses, each under a House Tutor who would be responsible for their welfare. This meant that there would be a spread of Forms One to Five in each House. Assemblies would be held by the House Tutors, although the Deputy Heads and myself would take the greater proportion. I particularly wanted the school to know that I was just as interested in the South Wing as in the North Wing where I was based. They agreed with my ideas although we knew that changes would have to be made when necessary.

The next thing was to appoint Staff. I would give all the present Staff of both schools the opportunity of joining the new school, although some would be disappointed that they might not hold their present Head of Department Posts. With this in mind, I met the teachers of both schools to explain the position. My Staff understood because we had been working almost as a Comprehensive School for several years. They had already told me they wished to stay.

The Grammar School Staff were a different matter. I made it clear that in our new school I regarded all departments as of equal importance and Departmental Heads, including the Technical ones, would all receive the same special allowance. I saw a few raised eyebrows and said that if anybody wanted to leave this was the moment to do so, because all the schools were appointing their Staff as soon as possible.

I had a few members of Grammar School Staff come and see me to say they could not work under these conditions and would be applying to other schools outside the Borough. They were mainly Heads of Academic subjects and I was pleased they made their own decisions. I knew then that I would have a Staff who would do their best to make the new school work. I quickly filled the vacancies and we were all ready to make our final plans.

I have gone into some detail about the change-over because I want readers to appreciate just how much had to be done. The only thing now was to see the parents of the new pupils and an evening meeting dealt with that. I knew many were not looking forward to the change and I knew some would go to Independent Schools and pay fees. All I could do was to tell them our plans and what we had done already. I think most of them knew from local newspaper reports.

It was a very amicable meeting, which ended with a tour of both buildings and a promise that I would be told as soon as possible of any changes.

It was about this time that something happened right out of the blue, which could have been a tragedy and changed our lives forever.

I woke up in the middle of the night and smelt smoke. At that time there was only Ada, Betty and myself in the house. Geoffrey was living in a flat in London with his cousin Michael.

I rushed out onto the landing, which was hazy with smoke, and saw it was coming from the staircase where it took a sharp turn to the left before joining the main landing.

Telling Betty to get Ada out of bed and into a dressing gown, I rushed downstairs imagining I could see small flames beginning to come through at the bend in the stairs. I switched off the gas meter and phoned the Fire Brigade, as well as our friends, Jack and Joan, only a few doors away. Jack said they would be with us as soon as possible with his car. Back upstairs, Betty and I helped Ada to the head of the stairs. She had not been out of her bedroom for years and could hardly walk but she was extremely brave and never made a murmur. Jack had arrived by then and we got her and our Labrador, Amber, outside and into the car, which Joan drove off.

The Fire Brigade arrived and looked for the spot where the blaze had started. I knew exactly where that was. Just outside our kitchen door was a room under the stairs which was built originally to hold coal – our main fuel for the house. When we had gas central-heating installed, this was the ideal place to put the boiler. Unfortunately, the workmen had lagged the pipes with the electric wires tight up against the hottest pipe and as time went by this had burnt through the wire's insulation and caused a 'short', which started the fire.

The Firemen damped everything down without making too much mess and we looked at the damage. Several of the stairs were almost burnt through and I still think of what might have happened if I had not woken up by chance. All three of us would have been trapped upstairs, with only a bedroom window from which to escape.

The smell of burning hung round the house for weeks while repairs were carried out and a new carpet laid.

As you know, I have always said that fate, over which we have no control, plays a big part in our lives. It does not bear thinking about

Chapter 13
CREIGHTON COMPREHENSIVE SCHOOL 1967

We enjoyed our Summer holiday in the caravan. I spent the last week at school seeing that we had done all we could to make it a smooth changeover.

As I drove back to school I noticed that a large Victorian house next door was up for sale. I was trying to give our 6th Form its own rooms where the 6th Form Tutor could be with them. They could use them for private study and even have some lectures there. They would still be expected to take part in all other school activities. Here was the answer, but I must find out if it could be bought by the Council. I phoned up my old friend, the Chairman of the Council, and asked if I could fetch her as I had something to show her. When I got her there she was as impressed as I had been and she would see what she could do. A few days later she told me that the Council was buying the house for the school. What a wonderful present to begin the first Term of Creighton Comprehensive School.

I know that all the Staff were determined to make a good start for the new school. We knew we were going to face situations we had never met before. I must say that pupils acted as if they had been there for years. Work had begun on the 6th Form Centre and we would be pleased to have the extra space.

It soon became clear that the need to move from Wing to Wing for lessons was a problem that we had to solve so that lesson time was not lost.   Maybe Timetable changes would help.   Another difficulty was communication between the two buildings.   The use of the public telephone would be an unacceptable cost.   There was a solution – we had to have a single line entirely for us.

The Science Department, under the leadership of Mr. Wiltshire, offered to try and solve the problem.   The GPO said it would cost £5,000 – the lowest quote was £2,000.   The Parents Association stepped in and said it would help.

I think this report that appeared in the local newspaper tells the story best of all.

"SCHOOL BUILDS ITS OWN TELEPHONE EXCHANGE"
Pupils dig trench for cable

When two school buildings a quarter of mile apart are made into one – as in the case of a new comprehensive – what do you do to bring them together? Build your own telephone exchange, lay your own cable from one building to the other, and establish your own internal system of communication.   That is what has been done at Creighton School at Muswell Hill – AND IT HASN'T COST THE RATEPAYERS A PENNY!   The new telephone exchange is to be formally brought into service today (Friday, 26 November, 1968) by Lord Belstead of the Department of Education and Science.

The school was formed into a new Comprehensive in 1967 from the former Tollington Grammar School and William Grimshaw School.

PICKS AND SHOVELS

The Headmaster, Mr. C.T.B. Loades gave the order to go ahead with the plan, and the Master in charge of Physics, Mr. Peter Wiltshire, commenced operations.

A small prototype was built in the physics laboratory.

The Parents' Association provided the money, and the pupils the labour.

One of the main tasks was laying the 60-core cable between the two Wings.

Parents lent picks and shovels, and pupils of all ages and both sexes, sometimes as many as 70 at one time, spent a hard-working two or three weeks at the end of the Summer Term digging the trench and laying and covering the cable.

A the same time, the exchange itself was being built in a small room at the rear of the laboratories in the North Wing.

Once again, much help was received from parents, in locating surplus and second hand equipment, and pupils soldered literally thousands of joints and used up hundreds of yards of connecting wire.

The exchange, basically similar to GPO installations, is switched on automatically at 8:30 a.m. each day and switched off at 5 p.m. At present, there are 20 extensions in use. Each 'subscriber' has a two-digit number. The system has an ultimate capacity of 100 extensions and will be extended towards this in the near future.

The Autumn Term was one of settling in. Everything that happened was new to some of the pupils – especially the ex-Grammar School ones. To them, so much was new; new subjects and new activities – many out of school.

I was particularly interested in seeing how the new 6th Form would settle in. I had asked one of my new appointments, Lionel Warne, to be responsible for them. He had come to us from one of the other Secondary Modern Schools, and I knew he was a bit disappointed that he did not get the English Head of Department post, but I had given that to a very experienced Grammar School Master.

Actually, I couldn't have done better. Mr. Warne was very popular with the 6th Form and encouraged them to take on extra responsibilities. He was also a splendid producer of plays and with him in charge we earned a high reputation for our productions throughout the Borough. More of that later.

Another thing we soon discovered was that we would have to look seriously at our Timetable next year. We did not have time for all the subjects we wished to offer and we had to find it from somewhere. Did it mean a six- or seven-day timetable?

At Christmas we made our usual visits to old people and had a Carol Service in the entrance hall of the North Wing. This was very informal with the choir on the stairs and the parents sitting below in the decorated hall.

There was a general feeling of satisfaction as we left for the Christmas holiday.

164

The Spring Term saw the completion of our telephone exchange and the appointment of a new Head of the Music Department. My experiences with the latter ever since I started at Grimshaw had been mixed, from the very good periods to the very poor. Our best time had been when we were producing Gilbert and Sullivan Operettas, but we lost that Master as he went into an Inspectorship.

The three applicants interviewed for the post, two men and one woman, had about the same teaching experience. The lady was West Indian and was teaching in Devon. They all impressed me, but 'Ruth' most of all. She was an accomplished singer, who would join the Bach Choir if she came to London. She also had experience with school orchestras, wind bands and steel bands. We had quite a number of West Indian pupils, who I was sure would be interested.

She would start in the Summer Term and by then I hoped to have the old kitchen, which was in the South Wing and no longer in use, fitted out as a Music Centre. Here, there was room for a full choir as well as the bands.

As it turned out, it was a very good appointment. It is strange how some adults are accepted immediately by youngsters and others, just as talented, not at all. You could feel and see the effect. Pupils began to bring in music cases containing their instruments for after-school instruction by visiting Staff. You could hear music coming from the new Centre during lunch and after school. It seemed that people just wanted to make music. It wasn't long before we were putting on concerts in the evenings, and there were rehearsals, with outside players coming in, for our first big musical, Oliver Twist, Lionel Bart's great success on the London stage.

The telephone exchange was duly opened by Lord Belstead from the Ministry of Education at the beginning of this Term, and we immediately felt its benefits.

The 6th Form, under Lionel Warne, was showing signs of great activity out of school as well as in it. They had made contact with a Junior School, which was having problems with its building and a shortage of Staff. Our 6th Formers were visiting in their own time to help with the basic subjects, reading and arithmetic.

They were also arranging trips out to suitable theatres in London and the nearby county towns. In this book, you will see photographs of such a visit. I was always invited to join them, and I did so when I could. A visit to 'Wind in the Willows" at a London Theatre at Christmas time will remain in my memory for ever.

My wife and I travelled with them to the West End. Each 6th Former had a youngster to look after and the excitement was intense. None of them had ever been to a theatre before, let alone one in the West End, and they thoroughly enjoyed themselves. We were in the gallery, almost by ourselves, and I shall always remember the constant stream of youngsters, each with a 6th Former, going to the toilets during the show. I'm sure some went three or four times.

The pleasure shown by the youngsters made all the planning worthwhile. I was never asked for any money to pay expenses – the 6th Form did it all themselves.

I had a Head of Department allowance that was not being used and decided this was the time to give this position to Mr Warne, for his 6th Form work. I told the Governors, and they seemed agreeable. There was just one snag. A Head of Department post had to be publicly advertised and applicants interviewed. I explained that I had not got a vacancy and could not have another member of Staff if Mr Warne was not appointed, but this had no effect. The rules had to be followed.

Oh well, why worry? There was no doubt as to who would be appointed.

How wrong can you be?

Six candidates, four men and two women, including Mr Warne, were called for an evening interview. As usual, they were invited to look round the school beforehand. From what I could see, they were all experienced, capable teachers who could do what I wanted – but we had a full complement of Staff already! Somehow, I could not get the Governors to understand this, and if an outsider was appointed I would have to lose a member of the present Staff. I knew who that would be, because Mr Warne would not want to remain. I would be losing one of my best teachers, who had proved himself so capable, and the 6th Form would be very upset as well. What would happen to their out-of-school activities and our stage productions? I dared not think about it.

They all interviewed well, and were asked to wait. We discussed the matters again, and then, for the first time since I had joined Haringey, I was asked to leave while they made their decision. In the past, it had always been: "Who would you like, Mr. Loades?" Before I left, I once again emphasized the fact that we had no vacancy for another teacher. It was Warne or no-one.

I was soon asked back and the Chairman told me they had decided to appoint one of the women. I could not believe it, and nearly walked out myself.

The lady was called in and offered the post. I don't know whether she saw the expression on my face or not, but she turned it down.

The meeting ended immediately – nothing was said about anyone else.

As soon as I got home, I rang Lionel Warne. The poor man was nearly in tears, and said he couldn't stay if the Governors did not want him. I asked him not to make any hasty decision. I would be asking the Chairman and Vice-Chairman to come and see me in the morning.

Next day, at my invitation, they both came. For the first time I realized that, politically speaking, one was on the left and the other on the right – so no problem there.

My first words were, "If I had enough money put by to live on, you would be receiving my resignation now. I haven't, and I don't want to go to another school outside Haringey, so I'm still here. Please explain what happened last night. You are on the verge of losing Mr Warne, who is one of the best teachers in the district."
Without any explanation, the Chairman said, "We shall be holding another meeting and Mr Warne will be appointed 6th Form Tutor." I thanked them as they left, and went to tell Lionel.

The matter was never brought up again. I've always wondered what happened to cause them to make their first decision.

It was about this time that another of the Governors asked me if I had ever thought about becoming a Justice of the Peace – a Magistrate. I certainly had not. He said that I should and, if I agreed, he would get an application form and propose me.

I was very dubious and asked him to wait until I found out if it would interfere with School work. Ron Fielding, my Deputy was already a JP and I knew he had one morning off every two weeks to attend court. He told me any other work was done out of school time.

I filled in the form – there was a good chance it would not be accepted. A few weeks later I was interviewed and invited to join – I would be appointed to a court in the area in which I lived. I must say, I considered this an honour and was pleased to say yes.

The court was at Hendon, not far from where I lived and I would attend one morning every two weeks unless there was an emergency.

After a months' evening course of training given by the Clerk of the Court, I was finally sworn in and received a letter from the Lord Chamberlain. I must say that 'the little boy from the wilds of Suffolk' felt very proud. I wished that Mum and Dad could have been there.

One does not enjoy being a Magistrate in the normal sense of the word. You see so many people who live in great difficulties indeed. It is not their fault they are up in court for breaking the law – it is just circumstances, which they cannot control.

On the other hand, there are many who deliberately commit crimes for their own benefit, with no regard for the feelings of their victims.

I learned a lot from my seventeen years in court – you are forced to retire at 70 –above all, perhaps, that JPs are there to help as well as to condemn! I was able to carry on when I retired in Norfolk and found it an excellent way to get to know more of the people of this lovely County.

I had one strange experience at Creighton, in this context, which I must tell you about. Soon after my becoming a Magistrate, the letters 'JP' were duly painted behind my name, which appeared beneath the school's name on the board outside the front gate. For some time I had received reports that a young man of about 17 had been hanging around the school grounds during the day. No-one had been able to speak to him as he always ran away.

I was looking out of my study window when I saw him arrive at the front entrance. He stood reading the notice board. I slipped out, without being noticed, went and stood beside him and asked, 'Are you looking for somebody?" He said, pointing to my name "Is that you?" "Yes" I replied, "Do you want to see me?" He just said, "Does JP mean you're a Magistrate?" "Yes", I said, and he replied, "I eat them for breakfast."

I do not know why I then said, "Well, if you give me your name and address I'll be round for breakfast in the morning"
He gave a startled look and ran off. We never saw him again.

I wonder what would happen today in the same circumstances – probably, I would be knifed!

This was proving to be a busy year, not only at school but in our home affairs too. When a house three doors away from us became empty, a very

English family - mother, father and teenage daughter – arrived. We invited them in for a drink, and it turned out they had spent years in Africa. The father, Jack More, worked for a big British multinational company which exported large amounts of groceries to the continent. He was within a few years of retiring and they wanted their teenage daughter to finish her education at an English Boarding School. They would come over for holidays. We said we would 'keep an eye' on the empty house.

Then came a surprise – the question of education was discussed and I said I had attended the West Suffolk County School. Jack asked when I was there, and when I told him, he said "I was at the East Anglican School – our playing fields were next door to each other – I may have played cricket against you." He was three years younger than me, so when he found – *Loades bowled More O* – in an old score-book, I insisted it was my younger brother! We became close friends, often going to the theatre together and spending holidays in our caravan. Jack was a member of the MCC, so Lords was a favourite for us to visit during the Summer, while Joan and Betty went shopping. They often came to stay with us at Mundesley after I retired.

At school, we were completing our first year. There would be GCE exams for the Tollington pupils as well as our own. It would be interesting to see if the change-over had affected the results. We had not been too ambitious about school journeys, but next year I hoped some would go abroad. We did have an Open Day which was very well attended. Everyone, including the parents, seemed to think we had made a satisfactory start.

One thing we had to do before we finished the Term was to decide on the new Timetable. We just did not have the periods for all the subjects we wanted to include.

I proposed a Six-Day Timetable. None of the Staff had ever worked one – and neither had I – but I knew the principle, which was: Monday was Day 1, Tuesday Day 2, and so on to the next Monday, which was Day 6. So, by then, Tuesday was Day 1. This was continued through the whole Term, gaining six extra periods every week. The number of the day, with a copy of that day's Timetable, would be on display in the Main Hall and in each classroom as well. Ron Fielding left for the Summer holiday with the task of putting it all together.

The past year had really been a "settling down" time, and as I left I felt we had made a satisfactory start and now had a solid base on which to build. It was an exciting and sometimes worrying time, but very satisfying. No Staff were leaving, which was a good sign, and we all, as far as I knew, were looking forward to the future.

Our holiday was spent in the caravan at Mundesley. We now knew so many locals that we felt very much at home.

It is impossible for me to follow the next years Term by Term. I can only give the outstanding events, good or bad, that happened as I approached my retirement. I had always said I would retire when I reached 60 years of age. I had seen too many Heads 'break down' with the strain when they decided to stay till they were 65. My wife and I wanted to enjoy retirement and do some of the things we had not been able to do whilst I was working.

(29) The Headmaster and Staff of Creighton Comprehensive School, 1967

(30) Creighton School North and South Buildings, London Borough of Haringey, 1967

(31) Creighton Headmaster with Junior School pupils on a visit by 6th Form

(32) Creighton Sixth Formers on visit to Junior School

(33) Creighton School orchestra

(34) Creighton School rehearsals for 'Oliver'

(35) Creighton School pupils constructing their very own telephone exchange

(36) Opening of Creighton School's new telephone exchange by Lord Belstead of the Department of Education and Science

(37) Creighton School 5th Formers at horse-riding class 1973

*(38) Creighton School
precautionary measures
against roof collapse*

(39) Creighton School in the national press, 1974
(Reproduced courtesy of The Sun newspaper)

(40) Charles Loades on day of his retirement, Creighton School, 1974

We returned after the holiday to deal with a new First Year and consider the exam results, which had come in while we were away. They were very satisfactory, but I knew that if I could keep the present Staff they would get even better.

The Deputy Head from the Grammar School was retiring this Term. For someone who had spent all her life teaching in such a school, she had adapted very well, but I am sure she was looking forward to her retirement.

I wanted to make an appointment from my own Staff, and I knew who I would like it to be.

Gwyneth Jones had been Head of the French Department at Tollington and had made the changeover very well indeed. She was in her late thirties and liked by both Staff and pupils. She had shown an ability to deal with difficult pupils and was enthusiastic about the future.

After my experience with the last appointment, I was hoping we were not going to have a repeat – and we didn't. We did advertise the post, but had no suitable applicants and she became the new Deputy. I know the Staff and pupils were pleased because they told me so. She had the ability to talk to the older girls as if she was one of them, but always held their respect. By a strange coincidence, when I retired she gained the Headship of a similar school in Barking. She could have taken my post easily.

With out-of-school activities increasing as well as the usual sports matches with other schools, it soon became obvious that we could not rely on public transport to take parties and teams around. We needed our own school bus. We would have to buy it ourselves, which meant raising

173

money by our own efforts. The school responded to the challenge enthusiastically and all kinds of fund-raising events were arranged by the pupils themselves, from raffles to sponsored walks. I remember my wife and I running round the grounds of our local Teachers Training College one Sunday in a sponsored event. When I say 'running', I should say 'we walked briskly' with what seemed to be half the school.

The money was raised sooner than I expected and we bought a Ford Transit Van with seats added, which could take any of our teams. Several of our younger Staff took the necessary driving tests for such a vehicle and it proved very useful indeed.

As with our telephone exchange, I have noticed that the enthusiasm is there if it can be harnessed.

I have always thought, even in my own school days, that sport is a very difficult subject to handle. Not everyone wants to play hockey, football, cricket, netball, etc., mainly because they have no natural ability for physical exercise. While agreeing it is healthy for everybody of all ages, it needs enough instructors to deal with all the different abilities. Trying to put a good natural sportsman to play with someone of low ability and interest simply spoils the game for both. The trouble is that schools do not have the number of sports teachers to deal with this difficulty.

With this in mind, I had looked for other forms of sport that would not require school Staff to run them. I found two possibilities. Talking with the older girls on the subject I found that several were keen horse-riders and went to a local stable each week. If I could persuade this stable, which was a short distance away, to take them during their sports periods, this would help.

When I explained the situation to the owner of the stables she was very interested – she did not get many riders at that time of day. To my great delight, she said they would not have to pay as they would be exercising the animals at the time and could groom them afterwards.

There was no difficulty in getting volunteers. These girls would enjoy their games period in the future as you will see from the picture in this book.

Golf was the other possibility and I went to the local club. Some boys were already members. The difficulty was that they had large numbers of elderly men and women who played in the afternoons and really there was no room for our youngsters. They were sympathetic but could not help.

Still, one out of two was better than nothing.

I would have liked to introduce gardening as an optional subject. We had the garden by the 6th Form Centre to use, but I had no vacancy on the Staff and there is always the problem of the Winter weather when very little outside work can be done. This was a move I should have to consider later.

This is a point where I must give credit to the Heads of the Practical Departments. By ranking them as equal to the Academic Departments, I am sure that those who took the Practical option soon realized that they needed English and Arithmetic to a good standard as well if they were going to succeed. Our Junior Schools must have been doing a good job, for I heard nothing of non-readers.

As extra subjects we could now offer Commercial, Domestic, Needlework, Cookery, Technical Drawing, Woodwork, Metalwork, Pottery, and Arts and Crafts. Everybody had the chance to try at least three of these without making them a special subject. Art and Metalwork students were working in conjunction with the College of Art and the Technical College on preparation work before eventually moving there.

I did not forget the academic work, which needed to be at a high standard if we were to get excellent results in GCE and GSE examinations. In the year that I left, we had pupils going to University – one to Cambridge, others to a Teachers Training College and many other courses of further education. I am proud of the Staff and pupils who worked so hard to get these results.

Just in case you feel I placed too much importance on Practical work, I once knew a very intelligent professor who couldn't change an electric light bulb!

I have written of the 6th Form out-of-school activities with younger, rather deprived, pupils. As I look through old school magazines, I am astonished at how much was going on outside lessons. As you will have gathered I was always encouraging this kind of relationship between pupil and teacher. If you have spent two weeks with your class on a school journey you will build up an understanding which is invaluable. Of course, just as in life, there will be differences, but the experiment is well worthwhile.

In addition to the usual sports both in and out of school, such as cricket, football - including a tour of Cornwall - netball, athletics and gymnastics, we had our own swimming pool and tennis courts, and a fencing club had just been formed.

Out-of-school visits included various parts of England for Geography field courses. There were also visits to France, Spain, Germany, Austria, Iceland, Yugoslavia and Portugal. You can see how much I was indebted to the Staff for giving up their own time to organize these trips.

All the time new courses were being suggested. One of these was Child Care, and it was very popular. I give the programme for this in detail to show how seriously these courses were planned.

Thirty pupils working in two groups completed the First Year. An essential part of the course was to provide work experience with young children, and pupils spent three mornings each in the first Term working in playgroups, and three to five mornings in the second Term in Nursery Schools, and two half days a Term at the infants and toddlers sessions at Fortis Green Clinic. All the personnel involved in these establishments were most helpful and, in a very large number of cases, asked our pupils to come again on a regular basis.

In their 5th Year, the pupils would be placed by the Borough Supervisor in special-care units, homes for the handicapped and other areas where tact and maturity would be essential. There would also be an opportunity to study for an examination if any of them wished to do so.

Among several outside speakers who came during lesson time were a Librarian to talk about children's books and the Headmistress of the Hornsey Centre for Handicapped children. We had not had time for other outings yet, but we hoped that Term to visit a centre for crippled people and a toy museum.

The time that remained in school was half practical, half theory. Practical work included making toys and clothes for children. The theory was a mixture of social studies, child psychology, hygiene and safety in the home, nutrition and many other topics which would give practical knowledge to these future parents and help broaden their perspective about childhood.

All the pupils on the course that year were very good with children and several hoped to make their careers in nursing or nursery teaching. Apart from this, many boys and girls felt that learning about parenthood was a relevant study for teenagers. We were pleased that boys had opted for the course for the next year because it is just as important to be a good father as it is to be a good mother and the playgroup leaders and nursery school Headmistress had all strongly requested that we send them some boys.

Our productions of plays had become more and more ambitious as the years passed. Practically every department was concerned in some way with costumes, scenery, lighting, make-up and ticket selling. We progressed from the usual school plays to A Midsummer Night's Dream, the West End comedy "A Flea in her Ear", and musicals such as "Oliver" and "My Fair Lady", which I chose as my farewell performance. It really was remarkable how much talent performed for five nights to full houses. We were fortunate in having Mr. Warne as the producer, with so much help from all the Staff. I shall never forget seeing Bill Sykes, when he is shot, falling from the ceiling of the stage to the ground. It was done so realistically that some of the audience were on their feet thinking he had slipped.

The Term of 1973, seemingly moving smoothly to the Summer holiday, suddenly had three things happen, which would have an effect on our private lives, and also the next year of school life.

First, Auntie Ada fell ill, and at the age of ninety-seven, died in the hospital. She had had a wonderful life, although confined to her room for a long time. Her mind was as clear as it was when I first knew her. Each day she did the simple crossword in the *Daily Telegraph* and smoked, under supervision, her one cigarette. Visitors to the house would not leave until they had talked to her and heard her stories of the past.

It meant that we were alone for the first time since we married. We had never felt ourselves tied down and friends were always prepared to 'auntie sit'. Still, it was strange to be without her.

The second incident concerned the school. It was June, and we were in the middle of External Examinations, held in the main hall of the South Wing of the old Grammar School, which was only a few years old. I received a phone call from the Education Officer saying that the building was to be cleared immediately on orders from the Minister of Education, and kept closed until further notice.

The following report in the School Magazine explains exactly what happened.

"Just after 10 p.m. on the night of Wednesday June 13th 1973, the roof of the Assembly Hall at Camden School for Girls collapsed. A few hours earlier, girls were rehearsing the school play. The following morning more than 100 were due to sit their 'O' levels. At other times the hall could, and frequently did, accommodate the entire school. It was fortunate that it collapsed when it did."

Official investigations got under way at once. The media produced their share of the speculation. On Sunday the 17th, an article appeared in the *Sunday Times* giving possible reasons (which turned out to be substantially correct) and drawing attention to the fact that the same consulting engineers had been involved in the construction of Camden School and a smaller building at Leicester University, which had collapsed only 36 hours earlier. The late senior partner had been a much respected pioneer of this type of building and, as such, had advised in the construction of many other schools. Therefore, it might be wise to make checks.

This sent Haringey Engineers and Architects hot foot to the files on the Monday morning. By lunchtime, they had discovered that they did, indeed, have one school of this type, so they set off at once for Creighton, hoping all was well.

Although they found no immediate cause for alarm, it was decided as a precautionary measure to close the South Wing there and then! This would provide for a detailed inspection and enable steps to be taken for any remedial work necessary. A day later, they received instructions to this effect from the Ministry!

Basically, these buildings were of pre-cast and site-poured concrete. Roofs and floors are pre-cast concrete beams, appropriately strengthened by steel wires and bars, supported by main edge beams and columns of site-poured concrete. At each end, a 'nib' projects outwards to rest on a ledge of the same width on the main beam. At Camden, this ledge or 'seating' was only 1½ inches wide – at Creighton it was 2 inches. Both schools were built before a code of practice was established for pre-cast concrete, but the minimum standard was set at 3 inches. In addition, 10 mm. diameter steel 'continuity' bars link the pre-cast beams to the main beams.

At Camden, some of the reinforcing had rusted through, causing the collapse. Before that happened at Creighton, steel props, hired from all over London, were placed under every beam so that each one could be inspected minutely.

We had the old Tollington building still standing and as soon as possible we could put furniture and pupils in there. Fortunately, the Summer holidays were not too far away. We hoped that the 'propping up' of the ceilings would enable us to move equipment for the rest of the Summer Term.

The Summer holiday couldn't come too soon that year, and we managed as well as we could until then.

We went, as usual, to our caravan at Mundesley and realized that in the Summer of 1974 I would be retiring. We had already decided that we did not want to remain in our large house at Edgware. Geoffrey was happily married and living across the river at Barnes. Most of our friends had moved away and we could not see why we should not come and live by the sea at Mundesley. We had friends there, and knew there were so many activities we could take part in if we wished. Besides that, Norfolk is a beautiful county with so many places of interest to visit.

Without really meaning to do anything yet, we were out for an evening stroll when we came across, on the outskirts of the village and overlooking the countryside, just the bungalow we would like. We wanted a bungalow rather than a house so we had no problems with stairs as we got older.

We arranged to look over the place and found it delightful – very roomy, three bedrooms and a large garden. The only problem was that the owners wanted to move next week. We knew that it would sell quickly so after discussion decided to buy it then. With no one to consider at home we could come down as often as we wished and get things ready for the Summer of 1974.

Our offer was accepted and we went home from our holiday very happy indeed. Matters had moved so quickly that our friends couldn't believe what had happened.

I went back to school with some senior Staff the week before we opened to see how much progress had been made. Work had not begun on the ceilings, but all the furniture and movable equipment had been taken to the old building. We would be limited in some ways, especially in Science rooms and we hoped we should not be away too long.

It was seven years since the school had opened and we had no longer William Grimshaw and Tollington pupils – we were all Creighton.

Many changes had been made to our original plans but the basic intention was still there – to give the fullest education we could to all – whatever their ability – and to do it in a pleasant atmosphere.

We seemed to be singularly free of disciplinary troubles. I put this down to the many activities the Staff and pupils shared together outside the normal lessons.

I had only used the cane once in my teaching life, and that was a long, long time ago. In fact, I was so disgusted with myself that I took the cane back to my room and broke it up. It was a serious offence I had dealt with, but I vowed that I would never lose my temper again with Staff or pupils. You cannot run a happy school by using violence but I also know how difficult it can be for Staff when they find control difficult.

Teaching can be a satisfying and happy job, or it can be hell! What other occupation is there where you are personally responsible for thirty or more children for five days a week? It depends so much on personality – which you either have or you don't. It's born in you, and if you haven't got it then I suggest you look for other work that you can enjoy. It is no disgrace to do this – just that you are in the wrong job and that it affects all Staff and pupils.

The Chief Inspector for the area came to tell me there would be a full inspection of all the Secondary Schools in Haringey in the Spring and it would last a week.

Curiously, I had never experienced an inspection in forty years teaching. Everybody was a bit nervous, but there was no way of making changes in the time available and the best thing was to carry on as usual if you were satisfied you were doing the right thing.

Work on the South Wing roof had started, and we hoped to be back using it by Half-Term. Actually, we moved back in before Christmas and settled down to our usual timetable.

For Betty and I, the weekends were a busy time. I had a friend in Mundesley who visited the bungalow each week to keep an eye on things. While the weather was good we would drive down on a Friday evening immediately after school and return on Sunday. The caravan would go into storage in October and I intended to look at it in the Spring and decide whether it would be worth keeping once we had moved permanently to Mundesley.

We moved mattresses and smaller items into the bungalow, and brought garden chairs inside too. Temporary curtains were hung, and we were quite comfortable for the weekends while we started decorating No. 4, Beckmeadow Way.

The Term passed quietly and we came to our last Christmas in Edgware. We had lived there for thirty years and would miss our Christmas celebrations with the rest of the family.

I had decided that I would inform the Education Office as early as possible of my intention to retire at the end of the Summer Term, to give them the chance to advertise well in advance. I had also told the Staff and the Governors, but not the school – yet.

The Drama Staff asked me what I would like for my final production in the Summer Term and, a little tongue-in-cheek, I simply said, "Oh, what about the musical, *My Fair Lady*?" To my surprise, this was met with approval – I think the success of *Oliver* had whetted the appetite. The

Music Department was pleased too. It had been an exciting year, with public appearances by all it bands and it welcomed the chance of inviting some of the students from the School of Music to join it for the show. It was good experience for them.

Music held an important place in the School Curriculum. It was much enjoyed by a large number of pupils under the enthusiastic leadership of Miss Burnett, with much help from school and peripatetic teachers alike.

A concert, for which rehearsals had been taking place every lunch-time for weeks, and included all types of music, from steel band to jazz quartet, wind band, recorders, various soloists, several pop groups and full orchestra, was much appreciated by a large audience of parents. As I said at the end of the concert, the programme reflected the vigorous musical activity that Miss Burnett had succeeded in establishing at Creighton. We now had a musical life of which we could be proud.

The steel band, in particular, had been very busy outside school hours. They had played at Finchley Methodist Church, Muswell Hill Youth Club, a school at Brixton and at Hornesey Schools Musical Festival. Everywhere, they were received with enthusiasm.
The inspectors came and went after a week's stay. They seemed happy with the way things were going and we had a good report later.

Time seemed to pass very quickly and the Summer Term was there almost before I expected it. We put the Edgware house in an Estate Agent's hands and hoped we could make the sale coincide with the end of Term and start our new life as soon as possible.

I told the pupils, at an Assembly, of my intention to retire at the end of Term. The news was received in silence. Obviously they had not heard anything about it. At least there was no applause!

The Headship had been advertised and the new appointment made. It was to be a woman. We all knew the name – Hattersley. She was the Headmistress of an Inner London Secondary School and the wife of a well-known Labour MP.

I did receive a request from her asking if she could come and see me. As far as I knew, she had never visited us before. She came, and I showed her round and introduced her to Heads of Departments. She came once again, in an evening, to a meeting of parents but that was all I saw of her. She was obviously an experienced person and knew exactly what to do.

"My Fair Lady" lived up to expectations and we had a wonderful week. The standard of acting was as good as any first–class amateur show I had ever seen, and the staging couldn't have been better.

With Mrs. Jones leaving as well, the new Head would have to make her own appointment. I hoped it would be from the present Staff who knew so well what had been going on. As far as I knew, all the rest of the Staff were staying on. It would be an interesting Autumn Term.

To me, the last week was lived in a haze. I seemed to be attending numerous "Good-Bye" parties and receiving numerous gifts and cards. One huge card I remember contained hundreds of pupils' names, including an 'Adolf Hitler'! There's always a comedian around! I still have the card, thirty-four years later.

On the very last day, I managed to get round to say a personal "Good-bye" to every one of the pupils. I admit to shedding a few tears when I returned to my room. In the evening, there was a Farewell Party given by the Staff and the Governors, which was again a sentimental affair for both Betty and myself.

At this stage, I must say "Thank you" to everyone I knew during those last seventeen years at Willaim Grimshaw and Creighton. They were very happy years indeed. We were in an age when education was taking a giant step into the future, without knowing what it held. Thank goodness the Haringey Education Committee was so supportive and wise to give us the freedom we needed.

I still remember my first day at the Grammar School when I was told, "You will take Latin for the first year, and if you are no good at it, change to Physics." The other difficult time was when I started in London and was being moved from school to school. In teaching, you need stability in Staff to make real progress, and I valued highly the loyalty that I was fortunate enough to enjoy in Haringey.

I ought not to mention individuals, but a special "thank-you" is due to my two Deputy Heads, Ron Fielding and Gwynneth Jones, who were exceptional.

I thought I would include here a copy of the Farewell Letter I received from the Chief Education Officer of Haringey. To me, it seems to sum up so well what I had really been trying to do throughout my teaching life.

We had sold the house in Edgware, the Term finished on the Thursday and the following Tuesday we said our final "Goodbyes". Now we were off to experience, as the local paper says, "The Magic of Mundesley." But that's another story!

THE END

Borough of Haringey

Education Service

Chief Education Officer
A.G. Groves BSc(Econ)

Education Offices
Somerset Road Tottenham N17 9EH
01 — 808 4500 ext 123

Please quote CEO/SM

26 July 1974.

Dear Mr. Loades,

I am writing this letter on the day that will be your last as Headmaster of Creighton School in session.

You and I have already spoken and take leave of each other, but I would like to place on record my belief that you have done a truly wonderful job in creating the Creighton Comprehensive School and that you are leaving to your successor a very fine school, in fact one which, in my opinion, can rank with any comprehensive school in this land as an example of the way in which reorganised secondary education can best serve the needs of all types of pupils.

Your immense gifts of organisation but perhaps even more of personal relationships with all people of all ages with whom you have had to deal have stood you in good stead in furthering the highly successful creative work which during the last part of your long career in education you have undertaken.

You will be very greatly missed in the Haringey Education Service, but you will never be forgotten. In retiring as you are as a young and fit man I do hope that you will find further opportunity to serve the community in the new area where you are going to live.

I have greatly appreciated our personal relationship during the comparatively short time that I have been in Haringey and would like to close my letter by offering my sincere thanks for this part of your work.

My very best wishes go with you and with your wife to your new life in a lovely part of the country and for a long, happy and most successful retirement.

Yours very sincerely,

Chief Education Officer.

Lightning Source UK Ltd.
Milton Keynes UK
25 May 2010

154656UK00001B/49/P

9 781845 493875